AWAKE INTO UNDISPUTABLE GLORY

Felix Nyemike Nkadi

BALBOA.PRESS
A DIVISION OF HAY HOUSE

Balboa Press books may be ordered through booksellers or by contacting:

Balboa Press
A Division of Hay House
1663 Liberty Drive
Bloomington, IN 47403
www.balboapress.com
1 (877) 407-4847

Print information available on the last page.

ISBN: 978-1-9822-4718-8 (sc)
ISBN: 978-1-9822-4719-5 (e)

Balboa Press rev. date: 05/20/2020

CONTENTS

CHAPTER ONE

My Soul Shall Arise And Prosper

The soul is the inner force and control center of our lives. It is the emotional energy and deep immaterial part that determines human existence. The origin of soul is found in ***Genesis 2:7 "And the Lord God formed man from the dust of the ground, and breathed into his nostrils the breath of life; and man became a living soul."*** This confirms that soul is the breath of God in the life of man. It embodies the divine purposes and vital force of God upon your destiny.

Breath of God is the divine nature and intellectual energy that differentiate human beings from other animals. The body formed from dust of the ground is meaningless without the soul.

The human body without soul is worthless, empty and miserable. Though man was formed from the dust, he possesses the privilege of divine nature because God breathe unto his nostrils and gave life to the soul. The most expensive material on planet earth is the soul of a man. ***Matthew 16:26 "For what profit is it to a man if he gains the whole world, and loses his own soul? Or what will a man give in exchange for his soul?"*** The human soul is a priceless treasure; it contains the destiny and divine ability. In fact, the Bible teaches that your soul is more valuable than any other thing in the world. But, many people ignorantly sell their souls for mundane pleasures. A living soul must be consistently positioned on the track of God for its destiny. God has graciously designed a unique glory for you to achieve on earth. The fundamental essence of life is to fulfill divine destiny. ***Matthew 26:24 "The Son of man goes as it is written of Him."*** There is divine blueprint that God has assigned you to fulfill in this world before you die.

Many years ago, I was having financial troubles and I went into fasting and prayer warfare. Surprisingly in a revelation, I saw myself appearing very rich and well fed, going to the most popular stream in my village where a large crowd gathered. I was preaching tenaciously and all the people were attentive as I declared the glory and goodness of the Lord Jesus Christ. Unexpectedly, I saw another person whose face and stature appears exactly like mine, sweating profusely and looking distressed, poor and confused. The Lord told me, "if you continue preaching the Gospel of Christ, you will live gloriously with comfort and wealth. But if you trust in struggles of the flesh, neglecting the gospel, you will suffer in poverty and confusion." I woke up that night, pondered on the vision, and decided to honour God with all my time. Since then, the Lord has bountifully released His kindness upon my life and family. God has continuously manifested His gifts upon my life and prospered me on every side. Glory be to Almighty God!

Every destiny is created with unique gift to make positive impact on earth, that people will see and glorify the father in heaven. ***3 John verse 2 says "I wish above all things that thou mayeth prosper and be in health, along with the prosperity of your soul."*** It means that your soul has the ability to prosper, it can either be healthy, strangled or sick. The state of your soul determines your true prosperity in the land of the living. The soul is your representative in the spirit realm. Most things that are abstract physically, like peace, health, joy or destiny; are tangible materials in the realm of the spirit. The soul is heaven's investment in your life, designed to profit your generation and give glory to God. For your soul to manifest the attributes of God embedded therein, you must maintain fellowship with God. When the soul is alive and healthy, you will enjoy the partnership of the Holy Spirit; and be established on glorious track for your destiny.

THE WICKED TRADERS OF SOULS

It is fundamental principle of the scripture that gift of God should not be for sale.

The most important gift from God is the soul; it must not be sold for any price.

"And when Simon saw that through the laying on of the apostles' hands the Holy Spirit was given, he offered them money, saying, "Give me this power also, that anyone on whom I lay hands may receive the

Holy Spirit." But Peter said to him, "Your money perish with you, because you thought that the gift of God could be purchased with money! (Acts 8:18-20).

The soul should not be traded in the market square of life but, the enemy in contradiction of the doctrines of God, have placed many souls on sale.

Nahum 3:4 "Because of the multitude of harlotries of the seductive harlot, the mistress of sorceries, who sells nations through her harlotries, and families through her sorceries."

The most dangerous sellers of souls are witchcraft powers. They sell destinies and families through sorceries, and have also vanquished some people to ignorantly sell off themselves.

The soul contains your birthright and divine blueprint for your life. It must be valued more than any expensive possession on earth. Do not devalue or relinquish your God given birthrights; nor sell yourself for nothing. Esau in the Bible neglected his destiny and sold his birthright to Jacob for a pot of porridge. The grandson of Abraham underestimated the gift of God and preferred immediate pleasure. Some choices caused by fleshly lusts are disastrous and preposterous; they truncate and trade-off people's souls. For instance, Samson sold off his colorful destiny to the enemy through his careless choices and actions. The destiny of Samson entered reverse gear and was unfulfilled because of his lust for Delilah. The way he ended up was not God's plan for his life. It is dangerous to take vital decisions about your life without consulting God. Your soul carries divine mission designed to benefit your generation. God is interested in the health and safety of your soul. But the enemy is seriously contending for the soul; he wants to cause disorder and abort the purposes of God for your life.

The soul of man can be exchanged for a price in the spirit realm. Your soul contains heavenly projects that will glorify God in your lifetime. The breath of God in you, embodies distinctive qualities that will decorate you with honor and greatness throughout your existence on earth.

The enemy have seen your glory, so he hunts your soul in order to steal, kill or destroy the investments of God in your life. So many souls are on sale, a lot has been sold while others are impounded or troubled. The devil has done so much havoc to the souls of men.

Generations of human race are facing untold hardship and deprivation from God's expectation for their destinies. So many lives have jeopardized and disappointed the purposes of God for their families and communities. Those sent as deliverers and lifters of their generation have passed through life unnoticed. As God ordained Gideon with power to save Israel from the hand of the Midianites; some people have tragically disappointed heavenly assignment on their destinies. The enemy achieves this disaster by pushing people into choices that besiege their souls and truncate their lives. The same Samson appointed from birth to deliver Israel out of the hand of the Philistines (Judges 13:5) was shamefully eliminated by same Philistines. Lust of the flesh can truncate a great destiny.

All forms of worldly lusts, hasty decisions and inordinate desires can place your soul for sale by satanic traders. ***Isaiah 52:3 For thus says the Lord: "You have sold yourselves for nothing, and you shall be redeemed without money."*** A person can be the seller of his own soul. Just like Esau and Samson sold their destinies for lustful and perishable gains; careless choices can waste destinies and cause untimely death. The dangerous effect of soul trading causes people to pass through life without using their talents. Their gifts fail to profit them in life. They have talents but no platform to use it. The devil knows the gifts will benefit them in future, but he stole them before they get to that age. Evil soul traders push them to wrong places, harmful relationships and fatal decisions. Negative indulgence for perishable gains can cause eternal and irreversible woes. Isaiah 50:1 says, "For your iniquities have you sold yourselves." That further buttresses that you can sell off yourself consciously or unconsciously. When Ahab executed wickedness against Naboth and was confronted by Elijah, the prophet said to him ***"I have found you, because you have sold yourself to do evil in the sight of the Lord." (1 Kings 21:20).***

The devil pushes people to disastrous actions that will damage their destinies and sell their souls.

One of the major work of darkness is trading on the souls of men; they steal and waste precious souls. These wicked traders lead men into temptation, regrets, depression and destructive habits.

When a life has been sold off, there would be destiny disorder, unfruitfulness and wastage. David recognized that some powers were seeking after his soul to destroy it, so he declared in ***Psalm 40:14 "Let them be ashamed and brought to mutual confusion who seek to destroy my life; Let them be driven backward and brought to dishonor who wish me evil."*** Jesus Christ is the only solution to the problems associated with the soul. You must fervently pray that the devil will not redesign or damage your destiny and your soul will not enter the dustbin of darkness. David said "He restores my soul." Many souls need to be restored from prison of darkness which strangles and demotes lives. When a person's soul is under attack, it causes disorientation, stagnation and frustration. I pray that the enemy will not pack dead vultures into your luggage of life; and your head will not enter evil pots in Jesus name.

THE SOUL NEEDS STRENGTH AND REST

Psalm 116:7 "Return to your rest, O my soul, for the Lord has dealt bountifully with you"

Just as its essential for birds to perch, our souls need rest in order to effectively praise and communicate with God. But satanic traders have denied and deprived the soul of man from enjoying the rest, it deserves. Jesus says ***"Come to Me, all you who labor and are heavy laden, and I will give you rest." (Matthew 11:28).*** The soul of man can only find rest in Jesus Christ.

The powers of darkness have consistently harassed souls with anxiety and dislocations in order to destroy destinies. Many people have become strangers to their divine original because the devil struggles to surmount and subjugate souls. Some people destined for greatness have been perverted to tow the path of shame and misfortune. Those who should help the poor surprisingly dwell in abject penury and frustration; because the enemy have stolen the gift that should make them great. Some are deceived into destructive choices that cannot be recovered. The enemy have lured people into cultism and wrong marriages that encumber and devour their destinies.

Another major factor that makes people become victims of sole traders is idolatry. The worship of idols will separate a person from the peace of God and sell him off to serve the wicked.

Judges 3:7-8"So the children of Israel did evil in the sight of the Lord. They forgot the Lord their God, and served the Baals and Asherahs. Therefore the anger of the Lord was hot against Israel, and He sold them into the hand of Cushan-Rishathaim king of Mesopotamia; and the children of Israel served Cushan-Rishathaim eight years." Idolatry can sell your soul into severe bondage and suffering in the hand of the wicked. God hates and condemn idolatry.

Anyone who depart from God shall be ashamed, forsaken and confused. Bible says "Their sorrows shall be multiplied that hasten after another god." The worship of idols can attract curses, tragedy and deadly yokes upon a person. Evil covenants and cultism will sell your soul. A soul in satanic market has no rest unless and until God sends a deliverer. The children of Israel had to cry to God, He sent Othniel to deliver them and they had rest for forty years.

When a soul is sold, he is sentenced to fruitless efforts, failures and oppositions from dark powers. Victims of soul traders dwell in the congregation of the dead, lacking the joy of living.

God hates idolatry to the extent that He warned Prophet Jeremiah to stop interceding for some people because of their idols. ***Jeremiah 7:16 "Therefore do not pray for this people, nor lift up a cry or prayer for them, nor make intercession to Me; for I will not hear you."*** Idolatry is abomination in the sight of God; it pollutes the soul and hinder answers to prayers. Flee from idolatry, it will corrupt your mind and defile your body. Those who forsake God are consumed in satanic fires on daily basis. Their lives are full of complaints, emptiness and worries, despite the money in their accounts. Jesus died to pay the price for our souls and to redeem us from the curse of sin, which is death. Do not join any occult group or worship any deity because of fame or material wealth, it will place your soul for sale in satanic markets. The devil hunts and buy souls to kill them untimely and disrupt their destinies.

The bible gave certain mysterious insight about the merchants of the earth in Revelations 18:11-13 where it mentioned about the commodities in the spiritual market which includes the "bodies and souls of men." You need the Spirit of God to open your eyes of understanding to the secrets of life. In fact, inestimable greatness and unforgettable possibilities will be released into your life, when you understand the mysteries of the gospel of Christ. Evidently, the spiritual realm controls the physical; and idol powers have beclouded and deluded the minds of many people.

Ephesians 4:18 "Having the understanding darkened, being alienated from the life of God through the ignorance that is in them, because of the blindness of their heart" Many people endowed with world-shaking virtues have passed through life unnoticed, wasted and unfulfilled.

Jesus asked, "What can you exchanged for your soul" It means that souls can be exchanged.

As we grew up in African villages in 1970s and 1980s, it happened that whenever an old man is sick, especially the idol worshippers and occult practitioners; children would be sternly warned never to go near their houses; so that the sick person would not exchange their souls. At times, when a child visits them during the severe period of sickness, the child would die within few days and the sick old man would mysteriously become healthy and strong again. Some study in deliverance ministry have revealed that occult agents trade on people's stars; exchange of glory.

Fervent prayer is necessary to shield ourselves against the activities of wicked traders of souls. Sadly, they slay the souls that should not die and save the souls alive that should not live.

If you despise the Lord Jesus Christ, the wicked hunters will take advantage of your soul, and suppress it. A healthy Soul enjoys the power of God, presence of the Holy Spirit and grace for unlimited testimonies. Your soul sustains your divine destiny. Do not trade your soul to satisfy your flesh. Living for instant gratification will rob you of spiritual blessings. Obedience to God will protect your body from becoming food to the terrible enemy. ***Psalm 27:2 "When the wicked came against me to eat up my flesh, my enemies and foes, they stumbled and fell."*** The fire of the enemy will not burn you, eaters of flesh and drinkers of blood will not feed on the carcass of your destiny. You need to intensify prayers against the activities and weapons of soul traders.

The worst enemies of men are soul traders. They hunt for souls and trade with souls. These wicked traders can imprison a soul and the person's life will be worthless, filled with disgrace and destitute of helpers. Some people live as strangers to their destinies because their original glory has been sold off. When the soul is sold off, the devil mercilessly controls and determines what happens to the person. He can afflict them with terminal sicknesses, suicidal thoughts, loss of investments and fear. They wallow in discouragements, strange attacks and ignorantly become slave to fake prophets. At times, you may trust a wrong friend who would betray and waste your resources. Once your soul has been sold off, unless it is bought back, you cannot be able to fulfill your destiny. The devil's occupation is to distract, redesign, impede and damage destinies.

The soul sustains the life of the body. If you transgress the commandment of the Lord, your soul will lack the support of God, and you will be subjected to defeat. Christ in you is the ultimate key to a healthy soul. As the earth revolves around the sun without being far from it, our lives must revolve around God, for our soul to enjoy divine rights, health and rest of God.

JESUS INSTRUCTED PETER "FEED MY LAMB"

James 1:21 "Therefore lay aside all filthiness and overflow of wickedness, and receive with meekness the implanted word, which is able to save your souls." It means that only the knowledge of God can save the souls of men. By knowledge, shall the just be delivered.

We are commissioned to spread the undiluted gospel of Christ in order to save the world.

Jesus advised Peter "Feed my sheep" but surprisingly, many Christian leaders and organizations are seeking material gains, despising the fundamental principles of the scriptures. Our Lord Jesus specifically warned thus "you cannot serve God and mammon." Mammon is the god of money.

Few years ago, one Christian organization called me to preach on a program. They had listened to my Audio CD sermons and were impressed by the teachings so they invited me as special guest speaker. I accepted to honor their invite. They told me the date and time of the program and also the venue, and I promised to be there. The next day, I was surprised to receive their call again requesting to have private meeting with me before the scheduled date. When I asked about the purpose for the private meeting, they said that we have to discuss on the pattern of sharing the money that will be realized from the program. According to them, so many rich people would attend the program and I should say things that will make them bring money. I quickly interrupted, telling them emphatically that I do not serve God for pecuniary reasons. The person exclaimed in shock "aah" over the phone; I had to immediately inform them that I will not come for the program anymore. I was disappointed because their purpose was to make money, not to save souls. We all face eternity every day, and we need to make daily decisions to please God, and not man. Honestly, the lust for money has eaten deep into Christianity of these last days.

Greed of some church leaders have made them neglect the poor, the fatherless and widows.

At times I ask myself "how many pastors will remain zealous for God, if tithe and offering are removed from church services." Many Pastors cannot operate in apostolic signs and powers because of greed for money; some of them conduct pseudo miracles on Televisions.

People can still give to the work of God willingly and cheerfully; if you focus on teaching the undiluted word of God and allow the Spirit of God to perform wonders in the Church.

Imagine if Simon the sorcerer or the woman with spirit of divination in the book of Acts were to be operating in this generation, they will become general overseers with thousands of followers because of signs and wonders. But the Apostles manifested the true power of God, stopped the operation of dark spirits and enthrone the power of our Lord Jesus Christ. Nowadays, most preachers teach how to make money and increase physical wealth without considering the health of the souls. ***Jesus says, "Man shall not live by bread alone but by every word that comes from the mouth***

of God" (Matthew 4:4). Bread sustains the body but the Word of God sustains the soul. Caring for your body alone will starve, strangulate and sell your soul. Jesus in the Bible gave example of a man who relied so much on his worldly possession. ***Luke 12:19-20 And I will say to my soul, "Soul, you have many goods laid up for many years; take your ease; eat, drink, and be merry." But God said to him, 'Fool! This night your soul will be required of you; then whose will those things be which you have provided?'*** Many people who presently do not have time for God because of money, will gather wealth that strangers will spend after their demise.

DECISIONS THAT SAVE SOULS IN FAMILIES

The joy and progress of some families are abruptly cut short because the word of God is not given the rightful place in the homes. The Bible advised that we teach our children the ways and commandments of God. ***Deuteronomy 11:19-21 "You shall teach them to your children, speaking of them when you sit in your house, when you walk by the way, when you lie down, and when you rise up. And you shall write them on the doorposts of your house and on your gates, that your days and the days of your children may be multiplied in the land which the Lord swore to your fathers to give them, like the days of the heavens above the earth."***

Some men of this generation have ignorantly traded family time for business success. The children grew up with perverted destinies, fighting their parents and living with hatred against their siblings, due to failure of parents to inculcate the fear of God in them.

We have seen several cases where rich and educated fathers were brutally murdered by their sons. Sometimes, the bad bargain you make can be so pivotal that it affects the rest of your life, and even have eternal consequences. Any child that was diligently trained in the knowledge of God will not be entangled in monstrous acts, to the extent of killing his parents. Peace among siblings and unity in families are secured by parent who devote quality time to teach the Gospel of Christ to their children. Some parents have lost their children to violence and atrocious acts prevalent in the streets. The environment has wrongly reshaped them regardless of morality and family values. There is no unity and love in some families, so much envy and strife, children are at war among themselves because the man of the house do not spend time with them. Your daily decisions and actions may constitute serious transactions about your soul and every transaction has a price either good or bad. What can a man exchange for his soul?

The future of your family, the health of your children's souls are divine responsibilities that God has placed into your hands. Your destiny can only be fulfilled if you trade your life for God's kingdom and righteousness. To be carnally minded is death but to be spiritually minded is life and peace. You will receive invaluable satisfaction if you make God the head of your home.

BATTLES AGAINST THE SOUL

Job 33:28-30 "God has delivered me from going down to the pit that I shall live to enjoy the light of life. Behold, God works all these things, twice, in fact, three times with a man: To bring back his soul from the pit, that he may be enlightened with the light of life."

The two facts identified here are:

1. The enemy detains the souls of men in evil pits.
2. God brings back our souls from the pit, for them to be enlightened with the light of life.

Jesus identifies the Light of Life as the privileged gift available to those who follow Him. In the book of John 8:12 Then Jesus spoke to them again, saying, ***"I am the light of the world. He who follows Me shall not walk in darkness, but have the light of life."***

The light of life is habitation of grace, rest of mind, peace and joy of the Holy Ghost. It is the glorious position where your spiritual rights are actively set with open heavens as child of God.

But the devil rages to devour the souls of men and lock them in evil pits. The soul must be delivered from satanic pits before it can enjoy the light of life. The pit of darkness is a place of evil spiritual exchange and altars; where wicked transactions are performed against the souls of men. Many souls are chained in ancestral covenants, and besieged by foundational wicked powers. For the soul to escape from captivity of the devil, deliverance is essential.

Psalm 124:7 says "My soul has escaped like a bird out of the snares of the fowler, the snare is broken and I have escaped." The freedom of soul is necessary for destiny to be achieved.

Many souls are vanquished, hindered and distressed by the powers of darkness. All troubles and painful experiences can be likened to a pit; these includes the pit of sickness, sorrow, fear and poverty. When the enemy manipulates your soul in the spirit realm, it manifests in the physical.

Psalms 103:1 "Bless the Lord, O my soul; and all that is within me, bless His holy name." When a person finds it difficult to praise God; the soul is already detained in the pit of worry.

A person's marital life can be manipulated from the covens of darkness; talents can be killed, businesses can be destroyed and certificates are bewitched. Satanic powers attack peoples' health and such persons suffer long on sick bed without solution until serious fire prayers are said for them. The greatest freedom in life is the liberty of the soul. When a soul is under attack, the person will encounter series of disappointments especially at the edge of success. There will be wilderness experiences in their career, subjecting all efforts to dejection and discontentment.

As God is interested in the state of your soul, Jesus paid the price with His blood to save your soul, the devil is also competing for your soul; he employs enticing strategies in order to steal your soul. The devil has knowledge of all spiritual laws and the specific penalties. So, he lures people to rebellious activities in order to punish and enslave their souls. The devil tempted Jesus with the agenda to truncate His destiny. ***Matthew 4:9 "All these things I will give You if You will fall down and worship me."*** If you desire to protect your soul from destruction, you must resist the temptations of the devil no matter the value of enticing gifts he uses to persuade you.

The amount of money in a person's account does not determine the level of peace in his soul. ***Revelation 3:17 "Because you say, 'I am rich, have become wealthy, and have need of nothing'—and do not know that you are wretched, miserable, poor, blind, and naked."*** This is the exact definition suitable for many rich men in our communities.

They indulge in cultism, adultery and all sorts of wickedness because their souls are naked.

If you neglect the health of your soul because of financial prosperity, that money will never give you the true joy and peace. The freedom and prosperity of your soul is higher than money.

I was invited to preach at a revival program, where I led series of fire prayers for about two hours, and the congregation prayed with utmost fervency. After the program, a lot of people demanded to see me for counseling. One woman told me that she was being pursued by the spirit of death. "What happened?" I asked her. She said that her younger brother is an occult practitioner, and has been killing members of their family through occult spiritual exchange for riches. According to her, it has become her turn to die and many strange sicknesses had befallen her; with fearful battles in the dreams. Her brother sacrificed his soul to the devil and members of the family were dying for the evil they knew nothing about. Just for the occult practitioner to increase his financial fortunes, souls were being sold. Dark places of the earth are full of cruelty!

Most occult practitioners die shamefully and prematurely after destroying their family members.

A person with material possession can be regarded as poor and miserable if the soul is sick.

I had to seriously pray with the woman to separate her soul from the evil basket of dark traders.

Wretchedness of the soul is more dangerous than material poverty. They can have big cars with censors but no spiritual alertness. By the calculation of heaven, many famous men and society women are dead. Despite their positions and possessions, their lives are full of complaints, mishaps and bewilderment. At times, you see some rich men engaging in ridiculous and heinous acts because the devil has taken control of their souls. There are people who cannot control some fearful thoughts and destructive arguments in their minds. Wicked demon has besieged the mind!

The devil troubles the souls of men because only peaceful soul can praise the Lord Jesus Christ.

Psalm 107:26-27 "They mount up to the heavens, they go down again to the depths: their soul is melted because of trouble. They reel to and fro and stagger like a drunken man, and are at their wit's end." A person's soul can be melted because of trouble. Emotions like frustration, indecision, fear and confusion are problems associated with the soul.

PRAYER POINTS:

1. Dark habitation of cruelty assigned against my existence, catch fire in the name of Jesus.
2. Every witchcraft agenda for my destiny, I destroy you now in the mighty name of Jesus.
3. Let the anointing for prosperity fall upon my life in the name of Jesus.
4. O God arise, save me from the controlling power of anger in the name of Jesus.
5. Every transaction of darkness targeted against my soul, catch fire and die in Jesus name.
6. Let every seed and fruit of the enemy fashioned against my soul, be destroyed in Jesus name.
7. Every worker of death, be cast down and be unable to rise in the name of Jesus.
8. O God arise and laugh at the plot of the wicked fashioned against me in Jesus name.
9. Father be my shield and buckler and stand up for my help in the mighty name of Jesus.
10. O God, be my Glory and the lifter of my head in the mighty name of Jesus.

11. O Lord my maker, destroy and divide every power conspiring against my destiny in Jesus name.
12. Every Power of the night working against my victory, die in the name of Jesus.
13. O God my father, arise in your mercy, restore my soul to your glory in Jesus name.

CHAPTER TWO

Justified By Grace Of God

Grace of God is the foundation of our salvation, the essence of our relationship with God and channel of God's banner upon our lives. It establishes our dominion as the redeemed of the Lord, the sought-out and the elect of God. Grace means progressive excellence, smoothness and elegance of movement. The ministry of Jesus Christ is the origin and pillar of grace which He freely gives to all believers. Bible says that "being justified by His grace, we should be made heirs according to the hope of eternal life (Titus 3:7)". It proves that Grace qualifies us to inherit the magnificent treasures of heaven. Jesus told His apostles that "everyone who has left his friends, possessions or relations to follow Him, will in this life have manifold with greater promise of eternal life." When Christians say "Abraham blessings are mine," it means that the abundant blessings and fruitfulness that God promised and performed in the life of Abraham will certainly be replicated in our lives". The bible further emphasized that as children of Abraham, we will always receive help from God. Grace keeps us far from oppression; and hinges on the compassion of God to abundantly release His kindness upon our lives.

To be justified means to be put right with God by grace through faith. Justifying Grace speaks and establishes the righteousness of God into our lives. The privilege that "in righteousness shall we be established" further guarantees that "we shall abide under the shadow of the Almighty."

As princes inherit the privileges of royalty and wealth of their father, the grace of God qualifies us to inherit marvelous benefits as sons of God. *Isaiah 54:17 "This is the heritage of the servants of the Lord and their righteousness is of Me, says the Lord."* Grace creates the platform for Christians to access the Throne and receive freely from God. It acquits and shields us from the accuser of brethren. Grace justifies our lives with the mandate of victory won at cross of Calvary.

Romans 3:24 "Being justified freely by His grace through the redemption that is in Christ Jesus" Grace of God activates, consolidates and revitalize the redemptive authority of Jesus' sacrifice on the cross for our sakes. It proclaims thus "No condemnation to all who are in Christ Jesus."

Just like being the son of a President gives you privilege like unhindered access to Government house; knowledge of Grace is essentially to appropriate the promises of God in our lives. Grace accredits you as candidate of the kingdom of God; which entitles you to righteousness, peace and joy of the Holy Ghost. Justifying grace approves, nominates and position us for excellence. It delivers us from the handwriting of ordinances, oppressions of foundational powers, and vindicates us from every conspiracy fashioned by the wicked. Grace legitimizes our divine destiny and appoints us to perform the works of God with wisdom that the enemy cannot resist.

Jesus declares in ***John 14:12 "Most assuredly, I say to you, he who believes in Me, the works that I do he will do also; and greater works than these he will do, because I go to My Father."***

Grace substantiates the purposes of God in our lives; it guarantees our protection and installs the kindness of God upon us. ***Psalms 84:11 "For the LORD God is a sun and shield: the LORD will give grace and glory: no good thing will he withhold from them that walk uprightly."***

The teaching of grace will open your understanding to the true ministry of Jesus Christ, the essence of his death and profits from sacrifice of His Blood; so that we can walk by Faith.

The power of possibilities in Jehovah the God of all flesh is freely endowed upon the followers of Christ, by virtue of His righteousness. The Faith that God hears our cries, fight our battles, intervene in our situations and disappoints devices of enemies, is established by virtue of Grace.

The manifest presence and power of God is active in our lives because grace is sufficient for us.

Galatians 2:21 "I do not frustrate the grace of God: for if righteousness come by the law, then Christ is dead in vain." The Grace of God is the fountain and source of righteousness; it is the end of the law. It releases the light of God into our spirit and permits us to flow with God's Spirit. Grace furnishes us with the resources of heaven and endow us with raw power of God. Apostle Paul said that relying on the law and commandment will make you frustrate the grace of God.

Grace epitomizes the Spirit of life in Christ Jesus which sets us free from the law of sin and death. The works of the law could not justify man because the law was weak through the flesh.

Knowledge of grace is imperative so that sacrifice of Jesus Christ will not be in vain in our lives.

Grace gives you the abundant life in Christ Jesus and mercies of God that over-rule judgments.

It validates your identity as chosen of the Lord and authorizes the glory of God upon your life.

Jesus is the source and giver of Grace, the author of unlimited possibilities of God to our lives. Apostle Paul advised in ***2 Timothy 2:1 "You therefore, my son, be strong in the grace that is in Christ Jesus."*** Grace is performance of God's everlasting love and faithfulness on our destiny.

John 1:17 "For the law was given through Moses, but grace and truth came through Jesus Christ." Moses used the law to guide and lead the children of Israel such that anyone who breaks the law would be punished, even with death. The law specifies punishment for offenders; it does not manifest the love or mercies of God. The law was our tutor to bring us to Christ for the faith which would afterward be revealed. The law gave strict instructions and commandments with specific penalties or sanctions to offenders; it did not recognize the weakness of natural men. But, grace is unmerited favor that is superior to anything that had been under the law.

Jesus Christ, the word and personification of God became flesh and dwelt among men to manifest his glory, and give us the privilege of His grace. Bible says that Jesus is full of grace and truth. He came to the world with abundance of grace. ***Luke 2:40 "And the Child grew and became strong in spirit, filled with wisdom; and the grace of God was upon Him"***

For you to fulfill the destiny that God has purposed for your life, the Grace of God must be upon you. Grace is the power base of our faith, the qualifier of the unqualified; it is favor beyond merit. Grace is the necessary vehicle to achieve the promises of God and fulfill our destinies.

AVAILABILITY OF GRACE

Titus 2:11 "The Grace of God that brings Salvation has appeared to all men." It means that once you accept Jesus Christ as your Lord and Shepherd of your soul, His grace will be released into your life. But, if you do not understand the great benefits of grace, you will not utilize this necessary vehicle for spiritual journey of your Christian life. Ignorance of the free gift of grace has caused people to fear the strength of their enemies, depriving the love of God upon their lives. Your help must come from the throne of Grace. When you operate on the platform of heavenly grace, all your desires and prayers will be granted with ease. Grace is the faith of Christ that has no impossibility in its dictionary. It ensures steady progress and victory for all believers of the Gospel. Grace intervenes and releases the help of God into your situation at the appointed time. 2 Corinthians 6:2 says **"God will hear and help us on the day of salvation."** Grace prepares, qualifies and attracts the manifestation of God's salvation upon our lives.

Those who do not acknowledge the efficacy of God's grace would always doubt and stagger on the promises of God. ***Ephesians 2:8 "For by grace are ye saved through faith; and that not of yourselves: it is the gift of God—not by works, so that no one can boast."***

Grace is unconditional free gift experienced and used by those who know the Lord. Bible says "That I may know Him and the power of His resurrection." Those who know their God will do exploits. For the word of God to perform the works and wonders of God in your life and destiny, you must operate in the power of grace. ***"Let us therefore come boldly to the throne of grace, that we may obtain mercy and find grace to help in time of need." Hebrews 4:16***

Some have pictured justification in this way: A person was accused of horrible debts, and was charged to court. After investigations, it was proven that he was guilty. The penalty for the offence is death but before the judge passed the sentence of death, a mediator suddenly appeared and declared to the Judge that he has paid all the debts owed by the accused. Then the judge rules that the accused is discharged and acquitted. Satan is the accuser; God the father is judge of the whole earth while Jesus Christ is our mediator. By virtue of intervention, mediation and sacrifice of Jesus' blood, we are no longer guilty in God's eyes. Jesus Christ has redeemed us from the curse of the law; He bought us out of condemnation and redeemed us from our sins. Christ took away our infirmities and bore our sicknesses, the chastisement of our peace was upon Him and by His stripes we are healed. The good shepherd paid fully all our spiritual debts; we are free!

This is the faith that pleases God, the confidence to perform the miracles of God without fear.

2 Corinthians 5:21 "For He made Him who knew no sin to be sin for us, that we might become the righteousness of God in Him." Therefore, Jesus Christ is our righteousness!

The awareness of grace will enable you to look steadfastly unto God, the author and finisher of our faith, as the only helper and last resort. His love towards us is overwhelming and boundless. You will trust God's word above all doubts, regardless of your prevailing circumstances. Bible says that righteousness was credited to Abraham by faith, not because he had done anything for it, but because he believed the promises of God. No one can be perfectly righteous by human effort or law keeping. You may have struggled so much to achieve a particular goal in your life; and have really given your best but nothing to show for it. You need this knowledge of grace to reveal the victory power of God into your situation for fruitfulness and realistic breakthroughs.

Grace will beautify you with the testimonies of Jesus Christ, which is the spirit of prophecy. ***Romans 8:3-4 "For what the law could not do in that it was weak through the flesh, God did by sending His own Son in the likeness of sinful flesh, on account of sin: He condemned sin in the flesh, that the righteous requirement of the law might be***

fulfilled in us who do not walk according to the flesh but according to the Spirit." Operating in Grace will make you spiritually minded and enjoy the true peace of God that passes all understanding. The Spirit of the Lord will fight your battles; He will defend and avenge you of your adversaries. When the enemy come like a flood, the Spirit of the Lord will lift up a standard against him. Grace will make you a reference point of honour, because it releases Godly wisdom. You need to operate in grace, it will strengthen you to victory on the day of adversity. Grace makes the resources of heaven available to intervene and deliver you from the hour of the power of darkness.

It elevates the believer above terror and establishes him beyond the oppressions of darkness.

THE POWER AND EFFICACY OF GRACE

Grace will keep you at the center of God's will for your life. It will supplement your deficiencies and position you for divine capabilities. ***Romans 11:6 "But if it is by grace it is no longer on the basis of works, otherwise grace is no longer grace."*** Grace is the operation of Christ-like faith, standing on testimonies of His victory over Satan and his agents. We are free from the spiritual colonization of the devil; and translated into the Kingdom of our Lord Jesus Christ.

We overcame him by the blood of the lamb and by the word of our testimonies. Grace is the spiritual authority of Christ accessible by us, to overcome obstacles and ride on the high places of the earth. ***Galatians 2:16 "knowing that a man is not justified by the works of the law but by faith in Jesus Christ, even we have believed in Christ Jesus, that we might be justified by faith in Christ and not by the works of the law; for by the works of the law no flesh shall be justified."***

Grace releases to us, the Spirit of life in Christ Jesus which delivers from the law of sin and death. Jesus Christ is the actual Grace that puts an end to the law of sin and death. He liberates our souls from bondage and give the light that darkness cannot comprehend. ***Romans 10:4*** buttresses that ***"Christ is the end of the law for righteousness to everyone who believes."***

The power of Grace puts an end to all ancestral laws, parental covenants and idolatry in your lineage. It delivers you from parental dedications and destroys evil patterns in your family line. Bible warns that ***"For if I build again those things which I destroyed, I make myself a transgressor." Galatians 2:18.*** Therefore, you must stand firm on the platform of righteousness that Jesus has benevolently given to you. Grace provides a new foundation for your destiny; it destroys the sinking grounds prepared by your ancestors through adultery and worship of idols.

Jesus is the new foundation of your destiny, the fountain of life and channel of glory for you; irrespective of any disabilities in your background. Jesus is our hope of glory, joy and salvation. ***"And I will pour on the house of David and on the inhabitants of Jerusalem the Spirit of grace and supplication; then they will look on Me whom they pierced." Zechariah 12:10.***

GRACE IS DIVINE VISITATION

Job said to God ***"You have granted me life and favor, and Your care has preserved my spirit." Job 10:12.*** We serve the Lord that changes times and seasons; He manifests to turn situations around. As He turned away the captivity of the children of Israel, God will specially appear to restore your health, finances, children and spiritually uphold His divine purposes for your life.

Luke 7:12-16 And when Jesus came near the gate of the city, behold, a dead man was being carried out, the only son of his mother; and she was a widow. And a large crowd from the city was with her. When the Lord saw her, He had compassion on her and said to her, "Do not weep." Then He came and touched the open coffin, and those who carried him stood still. And Jesus said, "Young man I say to you, arise." So he who was dead sat up and began to speak. And Jesus presented him to his mother. Then fear came upon all, and they glorified God, saying, "A great prophet has risen up among us"; and, "God has visited His people"

The visit of Jesus Christ to the scene of the wailing woman, changed her story to glory. Jesus said to her "weep not!" The shepherd of our soul visits to turn our mourning into dancing again.

When Jesus met the undertakers who were carrying the coffin, He touched the open coffin and the bearers stood still. Then, Jesus declared to the dead "young man, I say unto you arise."

I pray that the voice of the Lord will proclaim the resurrection power of God into every dead area of your life; including finances and marital destiny. When God appears into the affairs of your life, His light will terminate all darkness in your home and business. Jesus Christ personifies the spiritual light that terminates every operation of darkness. Any time He appears, dark powers and their evils works shall disappear on their own accord. Bibles says that Jesus has manifested to destroy the works of darkness. It means that Grace of God releases divine visitation which annihilates all satanic assignments in the life of a believer. As you appropriate these fundamental keys of Grace, your life will experience the dramatic turnaround that will surprise your friends and frustrate your enemies. The Captain of our salvation expects us to reign with Him in victory.

GRACE IS KEY TO DELIVERANCE

2 Corinthians 12:7-9 And lest I should be exalted above measure by the abundance of the revelations, a thorn in the flesh was given to me, a messenger of Satan to buffet me, lest I be exalted above measure. Concerning this thing I pleaded with the Lord three times that it might depart from me. And He said to me, "My grace is sufficient for you, for My strength is made perfect in weakness." Apostle Paul noticed that Satan had put a stumbling block on his wheel of progress. He saw the revelation of his promotion that God was about to fulfill glorious mandates on his destiny. But Satan also knew about the imminent kindness of God that was about to manifest in the life of Paul; so he orchestrated a hindrance to oppose the will of God in the life of Apostle Paul. That obstacle was a messenger from Satan with the assignment to trouble him. It was an attachment of confusion and charm of discouragement to retard him from doing exactly what he was supposed to do on the track of his destiny.

The obstruction was beyond the natural capacity of Apostle Paul so he went to God in prayers.

He prayed to God three times saying the same prayer point "The messenger of Satan, depart from me." Then, God answered him saying "My grace is sufficient for you because My strength is made perfect in weakness." The power embedded in God's grace will bring forth your divine original, perform the promises of God and silence the rage of the enemy for your sakes.

Bibles declares that "he that is in God is greater that he that is in the world." The grace of God strengthens, revives and delivers from every impediment designed by the enemy. I pray that any satanic messenger assigned against the beauty of your destiny, and powers plotting to waste your potentials, their agenda shall be summarily destroyed by the fire of God in Jesus name.

Grace releases the kindness of God into our lives. Even if the mountains depart and the hills be removed, the kindness of God shall not depart from us and His covenant of peace shall not be removed. It pleases God to mercifully intervene and resist the devil for our sakes. God will graciously refurbish us to achieve the great glory designed for us in the land of the living.

Zechariah 3:1-4 "Then he showed me Joshua the high priest standing before the Angel of the Lord, and Satan standing at his right hand to oppose him. And the Lord said to Satan, "The Lord rebuke you, Satan! The Lord who has chosen Jerusalem rebuke you! Is this not a brand plucked from the fire?" It was the appointed time for Joshua the high priest to receive blessings from God, an angel was commissioned to deliver the blessing, but Satan was standing at the right hand of Joshua to hinder his blessing. Joshua was clothed with filthy garments, which could be the iniquity of his ancestors. Then He answered and spoke to those who stood before Him, saying, "Take away the filthy garments from him." And to him He said, "See, I have removed your iniquity from you, and I will clothe you with rich robes." Any power from your father's house standing by your right hand to oppose your helpers, shall be rebuked by voice of God. Psalm 76:6 "At the rebuke of the Lord, both the horses and the chariots shall be cast into dead sleep." The angel knew that Satan was ready to oppose his mission, so he rebuked Satan in the name of the Lord. He further reminded the devil that Joshua was already plucked out of the fire, meaning that God has already singled Joshua out of any destructive pattern of his father's house. So, God promptly commanded the removal of all filthy garments from the body of Joshua and ordered that Joshua be immediately decorated with rich garments. God graciously changed the story of Joshua the high priest, revamped his ministry and beautified him beyond oppositions.

GRACE IS RELEASE OF DIVINE FAVOUR:

In the book of John chapter 5, Jesus met a man who had an infirmity for 38years at the pool of Bethesda; Jesus asked him "Do you want to be made well?" "The man replied "I have no one to help me" because he had only met people who were insensitive and self-centered. Fortunately, he encountered JESUS, full of grace and truth. In John 5:8-9 ***"Jesus said to him, "Rise, take up your bed and walk." And immediately the man was made well, took up his bed, and walked."*** Jesus is the only one who had compassion on him; Jesus is the source and giver of grace.

In the book of John chapter eight, the Pharisees, keepers of the law brought the adulterous woman to Jesus with the desire to stone her to death. But, the Grace manifested and redeemed her from condemnation. Jesus did not subvert the Law of Moses; He upheld the Law of Moses by saying, "Go ahead and stone her; but make sure that you are without sin. Because the penalty of sin is death and if you are a sinner, then you deserve death also." He was full of grace, and people who are full of grace do not throw stones at others. Grace comes first and then our obedience. When the Lord Jesus asked her "Has anyone condemned you?" ***She said, "No one, Lord."*** Jesus said to her, ***"Neither do I condemn you; go and sin no more." John 8:11***

Jesus was made poor for us to become rich; He paid the supreme price for our sins. By virtue of death and resurrection, Jesus has disarmed the spiritual rulers and authorities of darkness.

He shamed them publicly by his victory on the cross at Calvary. The evil powers and rulers of darkness of one's father's house would try to enforce the negative inheritances of sickness (diabetes, failed marriages, delays in childbearing, poverty, difficulties in education and incomplete deliverance) but, once you stick to the new foundation of Grace by faith in Christ Jesus, all evil inclinations and covenants shall expire forever.

In 2 Corinthians 3:3,6,17 Apostle Paul referred to Grace brought by Jesus Christ, as **Ministration of the Spirit**; and to the law of Moses, **as Ministration of the letter**. He further buttressed that the letter kills while the spirit makes alive. For as in Adam all died, even so in Christ all shall be made alive. Jesus is the resurrection and the life, for the liberty of our souls.

Grace releases the finger of God to perform the wonder working power of God in our affairs.

Luke 11:20 "But if I cast out demons with the finger of God, surely the kingdom of God has come upon you." Grace will position you in the Kingdom of God which is full of righteousness, peace and joy in the Holy Ghost. It makes you entitled to divine Inheritance of glory in Christ.

The power of grace is further enunciated in the book of ***Galatians 3:13-14 "Christ has redeemed us from the curse of the law, having become a curse for us (for it is written, "Cursed is everyone who hangs on a tree"), 14 that the blessing of Abraham might come upon the Gentiles in Christ Jesus, that we might receive the promise of the Spirit through faith."*** Faith is the spiritual platform to operate in grace, and achieve exceptional results beyond your efforts.

HOW WE CAN GROW IN GRACE.

2 Peter 3:18 "But grow in the grace and knowledge of our Lord and Savior Jesus Christ."

The same grace that saves us is what sustains us and enable us to grow. To enjoy the power of grace, we must decisively forsake sins and persistently serve God with patience and godly fear. You need to work out your salvation by allowing the grace of God to flourish and bear fruit in your life. The keys for sustenance and growth of grace are:

1. LOVE YOUR NEIGHBOUR: ***1 John 3:14 "We know that we have passed from death to life, because we love the brethren. He who does not love his brother abides in death."*** You practice

Love by being kind and compassionate to one another. Love is the fulfillment of the law, exactly as Grace is the end of the law. May the Lord give you the understanding to increase and abound in love for all humanity. Therefore, love and Grace are spiritual twin brothers that must always work together in our lives. God is love and whoever stays in love, enjoys the presence of God.

Love proves your identity as true follower of Jesus Christ qualified to enjoy the spirit of Grace. ***"By this all will know that you are My disciples, if you have love for one another." (John 13:35).*** To effectively practice love, we must forgive easily and show kindness to people in need.

2. SPREAD THE GOODNEWS OF CHRIST: The Gospel of Jesus Christ is the supernatural release of His grace as present help in the affairs of men. It is the power of God unto salvation to everyone that believeth. Grace is the message of justification and the pathway of liberty from the penalty of sin. The good news of grace is released by the saving acts of God due to the work of Jesus on the cross. It emboldens us to abide under the shadow of Almighty and trust in the refuge of His wings over afflictions and death. We are commissioned to spread the gospel of Christ; it will beautify our feet with dominion and excellence. ***Matthew 10:33 "But whoever denies me before men, I will also deny him before my Father in heaven."*** After Peter denied Jesus and a rooster crowed, Peter was discouraged over his own failure; he was very worried and upset. When Jesus died, Peter was frustrated, he returned to fishing but could not catch any fish. Then, the resurrected Jesus came, directed him and they caught 153 fishes. Grace came to restore Peter; commissioning him to spend his life feeding others, not in fishing. The Lord Jesus being full of grace and truth will restore you from falls and failures; and lift you to greater pedestals.
3. OPERATE IN FAITH: ***Hebrews 4:16 "Let us then with confidence draw near to the throne of grace, that we may receive mercy and find grace to help in time of need."*** The apostles were giving their testimony to the resurrection of the Lord Jesus, and great grace was upon them all.

Your faith will motivate you to lifestyle of prayer. Consistent prayers will help direct our steps and strengthen our faith in God. Prayer is the key for supernatural release of God's wonders into our lives. Your open heaven is waiting for your open mouth to catapult you to an enviable position with outstanding results. Grace will make you spectacular, enlarge your coast, and launch you into marvelous accomplishments. ***Acts 6:8 "And Stephen, full of grace and power, was doing great wonders and signs among the people."*** To enjoy His grace, all your trust, strength and confidence will be reposed in God. Keep thanking God always, and obey divine instructions. The power of Grace in your life, will melt every mountain confronting your greatness. ***Zechariah 4:7 'Who are you, O great mountain? Before Zerubbabel you shall become a plain! And he shall bring forth the capstone with shouts of "Grace, grace to it!"***

When the grace of God is upon your life, you are protected from shame and plots of the enemy. The power of Grace shields from failure; it will deliver you from danger and decorate your life.

PRAYER POINTS:

1. I receive the grace to fulfill my divine destiny in Jesus name.
2. Power of God Almighty, arise, transport my life to mountain of excellence in Jesus name.
3. Anointing to achieve greatness in all areas of my life, locate me by fire in Jesus name.
4. My father, arise by your grace, and destroy every obstacle to my fruitfulness in Jesus name.
5. Spirit of the Living God, appear, turn the table against my adversaries in Jesus name.
6. I receive the grace to achieve wondrous testimonies from God in Jesus Christ name.
7. By the power of God, I break away from negative ancestral inheritance in Jesus name.
8. Power of God's Grace, manifest and scatter every agenda of shame fashioned against me in Jesus name.

9. My Father, be a shield for me in every situation in the name of Jesus Christ.
10. O God, break the teeth of the evil Lion targeted against me in the name of Jesus Christ.
11. Every Power of the Dog working late at night against me, be dismantled in Jesus name.
12. O God arise and command all my pursuers to turn back in the name of Jesus Christ.
13. The sun will not oppose my day; the moon will not oppress my night in Jesus name.
14. O Lord arise, scatter by your power, all them that devise my hurt in the name of Jesus
15. The grace of God that establishes salvation, baptize my life and family in Jesus name.

CHAPTER THREE

Dominion Power In Your Feet

When God created man He said, ***"Be fruitful and multiply; fill the earth and subdue it; have dominion over the fish of the sea, over the birds of the air, and over every living thing that moves on the earth. (Genesis 1:28)."*** Dominion means total control over a territory; it is the authority to rule without opposition. Your feet are the weapon of warfare empowered by God to establish your dominion in the garden of your destiny. Feet are instrument of direction and deliverance. It is the vehicle for movement, enlargement, promotion and victory in life. God has given us authority over every other creature and we must strengthen our feet to achieve that dominion. ***Psalms 8:6 "You have made him to have dominion over the works of Your hands; You have put all things under his feet."*** Your victory is established when God makes your enemies, your footstool. Jesus explained the dominion power in ***Luke 10:19 "Behold, I give you the authority to trample on serpents and scorpions, and over all the power of the enemy, and nothing shall by any means hurt you."*** We use our feet to trample on serpents and scorpions and overcome powers of the enemy. Feet is basic tool for glorious establishment, liberty and honour.

The feet of man have strong connections with his circumstances on daily basis. A person's feet can be spiritually empowered, delivered, washed and beautified. Feet can also be attacked, hindered or weakened by the enemy. A polluted foot cannot succeed in the battlefield of life.

There is a spiritual link between your feet and your situations in life. If the feet have a problem, shame and disgrace is the outcome. There are people with blessed, strong and favoured feet. Also, there are plenty of people with paralyzed, tied and cursed legs; they struggle but no prosperity. The exact location of your feet spiritually is your real position in life. When Jesus says "Those who believe in Me, shall not walk in darkness but shall have the light of life;" it means that feet is connected to life. The feet can also be caged and manipulated by dark powers. Anything that captures or controls your feet has taken charge of your position and life.

Exodus 30:20-21 "When they go into the tabernacle of meeting, or when they come near the altar to minister, to burn an offering made by fire to the LORD, they shall wash with water, lest they die. So they shall wash their hands and their feet, lest they die." The washing of feet tends to life and peaceful existence in the land of the living. God instructed Aaron and his sons to wash their feet with water, so that they will not die.

A person's feet can be manipulated into stagnation, transfer of afflictions and untimely death.

Wicked people can use the dust from feet to summon a person back to the dust before his time, this is the secret of untimely death. Jesus told his disciples to shake off the dust from their feet against cities that refuse the gospel. Dust from feet can also be used as instrument of judgment. Your feet will establish your longevity, protection and the liberty of God in your life.

The feet have spiritual significance that determines what comes to a person and his activities. You need your feet to be cleansed so that you can be connected to the helpers of your destiny. When the feet of a person are spiritually tied, he cannot prosper. It is the feet that move you forward spiritually and physically. Any power that is attacking the feet of a man is attacking his destiny, possession and advancement. Jesus understood that the feet needs spiritual cleansing and he performed this in **John 13:5-10** "JESUS poured water into a basin and began to wash the apostles' feet, and to wipe them with the towel with which He was girded. Then He came to Simon Peter. And Peter said to Him, "Lord, are You washing my feet?" Jesus answered and said to him, "What I am doing, you do not understand now, but you will know later" Peter said to Him "You shall never wash my feet!" Jesus answered him, "If I do not wash you, you have no part with Me." Simon Peter said to Him, "Lord, not my feet only, but also my hands and my head!" Jesus said, "He who is bathed needs only to wash his feet, but is completely clean; and you are clean, but not all of you" Jesus washed His disciple's feet to manifest humility and inclusion power. The feet are required to walk in or out of locations and to access positions.

The cleanness of feet delivers you from dark judgments and entrapments of the enemy. To enjoy the liberty of Christ and walk in the divine calendar for your destiny, the cleansing of your Feet is ultimately essential. Jesus gathered His apostles and began to wash their feet. When Peter said "No Lord, you cannot wash my feet" Jesus said to him, *"if I do not wash your feet, you are not part of Me"* then he understood the necessity of washing his feet. It makes you to become part and parcel of the Spirit and purpose of the Almighty. Spiritual cleansing of the feet aligns you with the glory, peace and agenda of God for your destiny. It will empower you to tread on the lion and the cobra; and trample on the young lion and dragon on your path to greatness. Again, Jesus said to him, "you are clean but not all" because the son of perdition (Judas Iscariot) was there. CLEAN means to be delivered from perdition. It means approval for divine compassion and favour of the Living God. To be delivered from the attachment of evil powers of your father's house, and to walk out of the control of witchcraft battles in your foundation; your feet need to be spiritually washed.

Psalm 40:2 "He also brought me up out of a horrible pit, out of the miry clay, and set my feet upon a rock, and established my steps" The feet represent authority, dominion prosperity and establishment. Sometimes, instability in marriage and businesses are problems associated with the feet. Anytime you see animals attacking you in the dreams, it is satanic agenda to pollute your feet and cause demotion in your life. The enemy attacks the feet to defile people's glory.

Cleansing of your feet is very necessary for spiritual elevation that will certainly reflect to great accomplishments in the physical world. ***Ecclesiastes 10:7 "I have seen servants on horses, while princes walk on the ground like servants."*** Some people are severely dislocated, distracted and disconnected from the real path of their destiny. Spiritually bare-footed people do not walk into favour; they are denied their entitled benefits and they struggle in vain. People with bewitched feet are disconnected from helpers; they waste precious resources trusting fake and deceitful friends. They encounter unexpected blockages, deprivations and agony.

Some people stepped on charms or sacrifices and battles begin in their lives. Worrisome battles like wastages, misfortune and disfavor usually begin from attacks on the feet. You need the strength of the Lord in your feet in other to possess your possessions. **Joshua1:3**, God declared to Joshua, ***"Every place that the sole of your foot will tread upon I have given you."*** It means that when you enter into marriage you possess the good of the marriage. You enter into business, and possess the fruits of the business. If you enter into any city or country; you will possess the blessings of God wherever you are located. The spiritual authority on your feet will divide Jordan before you, and attract supports to enhance your success. It is the feet that moves you to fruitfulness and prosperity. I pray that the God of Might and Majesty will restore and empower your feet to enter into the garden of testimonies ordained for you, in Jesus name.

After Adam and Eve sinned in the Garden of Eden, and God was addressing Satan he said ***"I will put enmity between you and the woman, between her seed and your seed."*** The seed of the woman will bruise the head of the serpent, but serpent shall bruise the heel of the person.

The first place that the enemy attacks is the feet of man. When he attacks your feet, he is challenging your dominion, position and liberty. You need your feet to climb to the high places of the earth; and expand your capabilities. Your feet need to receive the power to destroy the enemies that oppose you from entering into your breakthrough. Then, you will begin to walk in unlimited possibilities and unprecedented favor from unknown sources. Your consistent obedience to God's instructions will cleanse your feet, spiritually. Regular communion with God in prayers, praises, study of the word and earnest show of love to humanity will cleanse your feet.

The bible says that Enoch walked with God and because of that he received great grace from God. The washing of feet connects you to the privilege of walking with God.

Genesis 3:8, the bible says ***"they heard the sound of the Lord God walking in the Garden in the cool of the day."*** Adam and Eve heard the sound of God walking in the Garden; it means that God Himself have feet. The Lord God was walking and His movement was making a sound but Adam and Eve hid themselves from the presence of God, among the trees of the garden. Some people carelessly disconnect themselves from their miracles because their feet have been attacked, desecrated or polluted by sin. Actually, before they ate the forbidden fruit, any time God comes to the Garden of Eden, Adam and Eve would go to fellowship with Him. But now, instead of walking to where they were hearing the sound of the feet of God, they walked away because sin has corrupted their feet. Your feet will establish your dominion authority in the garden of your destiny; and link you to fellowship with Almighty God.

1 Corinthians 15:22 "For as in Adam all died, ***meaning that all walked away from the presence of God,*** even so in Christ all shall be made alive, ***meaning that ALL shall connect to the fellowship of Christ, in the goodness and the communion of God,*** for He must reign till he has put enemies under his feet." When you walk with God, He strengthens your feet to dominate the temple of your destiny and subjugate all oppositions to become your footstool. God will reign in our lives until all our enemies are put under our feet. We shall not build for strangers to inhabit; God will make his ways to be established in our lives. Any power that is pushing you away from your blessing shall suddenly receive the fire of destruction from heaven. Any evil covenant or decree of darkness from your foundation pushing you away from divine helpers shall be scattered.

Any attack on your feet is oppression against your peace. ***Roman 16:20*** the bible says that ***"God of peace shall bruise Satan under our feet."*** When the Lord Jesus puts Satan under your feet, you will receive peace in abundance. Blessings shall come to you without struggle; you will obtain wonderful testimonies. You must win battles and overcome obstacles before you possess divine heritage for your feet. You need to understand that your feet are instrument of your direction and deliverance. Unfortunately, some people rub satanic creams on their legs, making covenants with demonic powers that attack their feet. The feet are vital for progress and restorations in your life. Spiritually cleansed feet are blessed with divine empowerment to defeat foundational dragon. Breakthroughs and exalted positions first settles in the spirit realm before it manifests physically.

REASONS WHY YOU NEED TO WASH YOUR FEET

DIVINE DIRECTION: ***Luke 1:79 "To give light to those who sit in darkness and the shadow of death, to guide our feet into the way of peace."*** When your feet are spiritually cleansed, you will not walk into troubles or dangers, and you will escape evil traps that the enemy had set against you. The beauty of your feet will save you from pollution and corruptions of the world. God will not allow my foot to slip, my keeper shall not slumber. You will be directed by God and connected to the helpers of your destiny. With your feet you ascend the stairs of excellence. Sometimes a dream about feet indicates the need to support some areas of your life, you consider important. The purpose of dominion power of your feet is to excel and make your enemies your foot stool. David declared, the LORD said unto my Lord; sit down at my right hand side until I make your enemies your foot stool. This means dominion power on the feet. Some people may discover that they keep walking into trouble; some are always at the wrong place thereby causing problems for them; many have found it difficult to move forward in life.

Your feet are the instrument of your promotion: You need your feet to connect yourself with the princes of the earth; the great leaders in your generation. ***1 Samuel 2:8 "God raises the poor from the dust and lifts the beggar from the ash heap, to set them among princes and make them inherit the throne of glory."*** You need your feet to climb the ladder of greatness. The anointing of liberty on your feet will make opportunities work for you. The enemy has defiled some feet to hinder them from entering into their blessings. Such people will ignorantly move away from their helpers; at times they fail at the edge of success and loose golden opportunities.

Your feet are essential for victory: With your feet you receive the power to overcome challenges and win the battles of life. The bible says "***replenish the earth and subdue it."*** You need the power of God to subdue any dark power in your foundation. The Psalmist said "the lion and the dragon have I trampled under my feet." The authority of God in your feet will promote you above conspiracy, confusions and condemnations. You will destroy the powers of strongman assigned against your family. Jesus defeated principalities and powers and gave us the authority to overcome satanic oppressions. ***Bible says "You defeat the enemy by putting your legs on the neck of the enemy" Joshua 10:24.*** The victory power of God is positioned in your feet to crush the head of every serpent or scorpions challenging your destiny. Satanic immigration officers at the gate of your breakthroughs shall be trodden down by the power of God. All problems and struggles of life are the knees that must bow at the mention of the name 'JESUS'.

We are victorious in Christ! God will guard the feet of His saints; and make us His battle axe.

The feet carry your strength in the place of prayer, strong feet are never weak during prayer warfare. But, if your feet are weak, you will always plan to pray but will not be able to pray. When the person is praying, all the problems will gather in his head and minds, so he will not concentrate. The enemy is interested on capturing the feet in order to manipulate your movements and control your time. Sometimes, people encounter strong pursuers attacking them in the dream. They run like prey until they wake up, sweating and panting; because their feet are besieged by dark powers. Most afflictions and disorientations are dark plantations in the dream.

Any water that captures the feet of a person can drown him; and irrespective of a person's height, any pit that ensnares the feet can swallow him.

Jeremiah 5:26 'For among My people are found wicked men; they lie in wait as one who sets snares; they set a trap; they catch men." These wicked agents dig evil pits and set dangerous traps to catch men; but the sanctification of God on your feet will preserve you. The monstrous diggers will be swallowed in their own pit. Any wicked trap set against you in order to capture your feet shall be scattered by the fire of God. When a man's way pleases the Lord, his enemies will become his friends. Your way pleases the Lord, when He commands all creatures to obey His Will and purposes for your life. The principalities and witchcraft powers in your father's house shall begin to obey the instruction **'hear ye him'.** You need to pray to the level that powers of darkness will have no other option than to leave you alone. The kingdom of Heaven allows violent prayers and the violent, possesses their rightful destiny by force. The Lord said my ministers shall be made flame of fire. When you become that fire, your feet are delivered from any agenda of Satan; and from attack of dark powers. They shall begin to fear you because when you pray, you send confusions into the camp of enemies. You must fervently pray to deliver your feet from ancestral curses and dark covenants. Summons of demotion will fail for your sake; instead of you to come down, let fire descend and consume all the powers demanding your relegation. The name of the Lord is strong tower; fervent prayers will establish your feet under the protective canopy of the Lord's name.

THE ADVANTAGES OF BEAUTIFUL FEET

The beauty of your feet will reflect on your physical destiny. ***Romans 10:15 "How beautiful are the feet of those who preach the gospel of peace, who bring glad tidings of good things!"***

The feet of those who preach the gospel of peace are beautiful. There are some feet that have negative messages. Spreading the gospel of peace means to convert sinners to accept Jesus Christ, as the Lord and savior of their souls. It means to ensure the peace of God in your home, office, Church, relationships and among friends. Speak the truth to create peaceful existence among brothers, bring people to the righteousness of Christ and the beauty of God will shine upon your feet. Beautiful feet shall not walk into the horrible traps or pit of the enemy; they live above shame and prosper beyond limitations. Beautiful feet walk in the light, compassion and love of God. The enemy tries to paralyze the feet and render it feeble spiritually in order to subjugate and confuse the person.

Some feet stumble on their way to success. ***Psalm 56:13 "For You have delivered my soul from death, indeed my feet from stumbling, so that I may walk before God in the light of the living."*** Your feet are spiritual transporters of the glorious virtues of your destiny. Some feet are ugly spiritually, they do good things for people and same people would pay them back in bad coin, most times it is not their faults. They walk into bad relationships, they do business with wicked people who cheat, confuse and cause problems for them. I pray that the power of God will beautify your feet, and deliver you from regrettable circumstances; you will not enter into destructive relationships in Jesus name. Beautiful feet walk into unexpected favour and great testimonies. God will decorate your feet for honour and breakthroughs. People will only remember your good deeds; they will not condemn you by your mistakes and you will receive help from unanticipated sources. ***The word of God is a lamp to my feet and a light to my path (Psalms 119:105).***

I hereby outline the four advantages of beautiful feet, so you can take necessary actions to keep your feet in the light and beauty of God.

1. **Beauty of your feet will protect you from walking into unexpected evil attacks.** At times people accidentally encounter tragedies that are not planned for them. They will be somewhere; somebody will aim another person to strike, but will strike them mistakenly. Some are victims of stray bullets because their feet are manipulated by the powers of darkness. Some people have ignorantly walked into evil nets; and bitterly experience misfortunes that ordinarily should not come to them. Unfortunately, innocent people go to prison for offences that they did not commit. ***Psalm 25:15 "Mine eyes are ever toward the LORD; for he shall pluck my feet out of the net."*** I pray that you will not use your feet to enter into problems in Jesus name. Declare this prayer: ***"Any evil deposit that entered into my feet, I shake you out by fire in the name of Jesus.*** Shake out poverty, regrets, shame, disappointments, sicknesses and affliction. Shake your legs while praying this prayer!
2. ***Beautiful Feet overcome reproach: Joshua 5:9 Then the Lord said to Joshua, "This day I have rolled away the reproach of Egypt from you."*** Reproach means severe oppositions; powers standing against your liberty. There are people that unexpectedly hit their legs on stone in the dream and they wake up to see disappointment in their homes. God will arise for your sake, and roll away any stone that the enemy has placed on your way to prosperity.

Psalm 91:11 ***"For He shall give His angels charge over you, to keep you in all your ways. In their hands they shall bear you up, lest you dash your foot against a stone.".*** The stone of reproach is the program of darkness designed to limit your life. They are powers of reproach standing on the curses, covenants, and dedications of your parents or ancestors to stop the glory of your destiny. What is evil stone? The stone is the power that helped your parents when they were worshiping idols and is now demanding your worship, standing on the promises that your parents made concerning you. You will trample upon them by fire.

3. **Beautiful feet shall not be visited with evil:** There are some people that strangers suddenly visits in the dream to harass or torment them. When that stranger enters, they will be weak and feel like something is pressing them down. In the physical life, they found it difficult to go to church services, because the enemy is attacking their feet. The psalmist declared that he was very happy when they said let us go to the house of God. People with cleansed and beautiful feet will be passionate to serve God. They will have the desire to attend programs of praises and prayers to God. Any grip of darkness against your feet, stopping you from entering into your breakthrough, shall be roasted by fire in Jesus name.
4. **Beautiful Feet are empowered to cross their personal Jordan:** You need the power of God on your feet to cross your personal Jordan. Remember, when Elijah gave the double portion of anointing to Elisha; the first place he manifested that anointing was on Jordan river. When he wanted to cross Jordan, he said "where is the Lord God of Elijah?" Every human being has a personal Jordan. Before the children of Israel entered into their promise land, it was a time for them to cross river Jordan.

   On the day they were to cross Jordan, the power of God entered into their feet. It was not the rod now because they were entering into their possession. Moses' rod was instrument of deliverance; the rod only worked to divide red sea and deliver them from strong enemy. For you to enter into the promise of God for your destiny, the power of God must work through your feet to divide your private Jordan. The bible says that when the priests that carried the ark of the Lord put their feet on the water, waters of the Jordan were cut off, the waters that come down from upstream stood as a heap. ***Joshua 3:17 "Then the priests who bore the ark of the covenant of the LORD stood firm on dry ground in the midst of the Jordan; and all Israel crossed over on dry ground, until all the people had crossed completely over the Jordan."*** Your feet shall command open doors to your promised land. It will magnetize people to go out of their ways to bless you. Your life will never remain the same, when the power of God enters your feet. It will command gifts from high places into your bosom; and release healing into your body. Your lines will be fallen on pleasant places; and you will begin to make good use of your time. Anything you do prospers beyond expectations because the ancestral gates of limitations has been lifted away.

ANOINTING POWER OF POSSESSION IN THE FEET

Anointing breaks evil yokes on the feet. The anointing will make opportunities work for you. Bewitched legs walk into sorrow, regret and untimely death; some people walked into shame, wastage and troubles. The grave that does not capture a person's feet will not bury him.

Any evil arrow that entered into your life through your feet, shall bounce back to the senders.

Our spiritual inheritance in Christ includes that ***"no weapon formed against us shall prosper".*** Your feet shall be led by the Spirit of God, and any sacrifice of darkness remotely controlling your movements shall expire by fire. The righteousness of God is declaration of war against opposing powers. It cuts asunder the cords of wicked and recompense with tribulations, all powers that trouble you. Any power that stops your feet spiritually, will eventually stop you from achieving meaningful progress in your business investments; you must pray to stop them.

The Bible declares that God has given His angels the duty to protect our feet from obstructions. And, we shall destroy every dragon and strongman from our foundation working against our success. ***Psalm 91:13 "You shall tread upon the lion and the cobra, the young lion and the serpent you***

shall trample underfoot." The anointing of God on your feet will break every yoke of ancestral bondages. Foundational serpents are swallowing powers that bury blessings and ridicule virtues in families. God will burst the belly of the dragon and cause it to vomit riches and talents that it had swallowed. Anointed feet receive assistance of heavenly angels; they see the end of their enemies.

Like Joshua, they walk in victory, humility, strength and confidence. People with anointed feet seek the presence of God and abide in His covenant. They are not proud; they fear God and have compassion for the poor and needy. They are the meek of the earth with spiritual immunity to inherit the restoration of long term ancestral wealth. Anointed Feet walk towards their helpers and their helpers also walk to their location, ready to bless them. You will walk and locate your place of glory, favor and profitable opportunities. God will raise men to support and promote you. Samuel walked to Jesse's house to anoint David. The person that will anoint you shall come to your own house. Peter and John walked to the beautiful gate, and performed great miracle.

A man was at the beautiful gate but his life was not beautiful because of the problem in his feet. But when the people that carry the power of God encountered him, they declared to him saying ***"silver and gold have I none but what I have will I give unto you, stand up and walk."***

Jesus walked the way of blind Bartimeus and gave him sight. Saul located Prophet Samuel and he received anointing that made him the King. God will regulate your feet to the miraculous encounter that will change your life forever.

When Zacchaeus climbed the tree with his feet, he received divine identification and salvation. One day, Zacchaeus took a step that is not ordinary, he climbed the Sycamore tree and Jesus singled him out for honour. Jesus said to him ***""Zacchaeus, make haste and come down, for today I must stay at your house."*** Jesus went to his house make this wonderful declaration to Zacchaeus ***"Today salvation has come to this house, because he also is a son of Abraham" Luke 19:9*** Your feet shall move you to the salvation of the Almighty God.

In John chapter 12, Mary of Bethany anointed Jesus' feet presumably in gratitude for raising her brother Lazarus from the dead. The feet define performances of strong decisions and actions.

To put your foot down, means to stand on your decision. To foot the bill means to cater for the expenses. Any altar of darkness on assignment to cripple your feet shall be demolished by fire.

POWERS THAT WORKS AGAINST THE FEET

These are powers on assignment, unrepentantly against the feet of man.

1. **Evil dogs**: Their work is to crucify. They search for your mistakes or weaknesses and use it to crucify you. The bible calls them dogs. ***Psalm 22:16 "For dogs have surrounded me; the congregation of the wicked has enclosed me. They pierced my hands and my feet."*** The bible calls them band of evil men, congregation of the wicked. They are dogs in human form. They look for your faults and deficiencies and use it to strike against you. The Psalmist said they pierced his hand and feet. They crucify, condemn, judge and punish people without hearing from the victim. Any power on assignment to crucify you shall be destroyed by fire. The bible again called them dogs in ***Philippians 3:2*** *Apostle Paul said* ***"beware of dogs, beware of workers of iniquity."*** David in Psalms called them **congregation of the wicked** and Apostle Paul in the book of Philippians referred to them as **workers of iniquity.** They are not tired of doing evil. Even if you are crying, it does not change or pacify them. Their utmost desire is to see the obituary of the victim. Again, the Bible identified them as dogs in ***Mathew 7:6*** *Jesus says,* ***"Do not give what is holy to the dogs; nor cast your pearls before swine"*** What do they do? He said that after they have received the gifts from you ***"lest they trample them under their feet, and turn and tear you in pieces."*** You will do your best for them but they will rubbish your generosity and turn around to tarnish your image. Their mission is for you to end in shame. They wickedly use your kindness to criticize you.

One day, some Pharisees came to Jesus Christ, they told him, you need to leave here now because Herod wants to kill you. Jesus replied them in ***Luke 13:32*** saying ***"Go, tell that fox, 'Behold, I cast out demons and perform cures today and tomorrow, and the third day I shall be perfected.'"*** He referred to Herod as Fox, the same family with dogs. Their agenda is to kill and destroy like Satan, their father. God will arise and deliver you from any evil ruler that has authority over you, and is wickedly using it to strangulate your life; God will abort their atrocious agenda.

2. **The foot of pride**: ***Psalm 36:11 "Let not the foot of pride come against me, and let not the hand of the wicked drive me away."*** The foot of pride are the people who says 'over their dead body'. They are the people that use the phrase 'I will make sure'. They pride themselves in wickedness, saying "they will make sure you do not get to glorious level." They proclaim wicked readiness to ensure that you will not succeed. A young boy many years ago was doing much better than his peers, one day a witch sent his son to speak to the boy. He went to the boy and said 'I am your mate but you are doing well above all your mates, ***you will not finish your education.***' That power continued to follow the boy until he learnt to pray some fire prayers. Any evil decree by the foot of pride against your life shall be revoked by the power of God. The feet of pride are powers on assignment to stop your joy. They are on assignment to turn the person's day of glory to a day of shame. You need the intervention of the Spirit of God to stop such powerful enemies. ***Psalm 59:19 "…when the enemy come like a flood, the Spirit of the Lord shall lift up a standard against them."*** Any power that have the wherewithal to oppress your destiny shall be destroyed by fire.
3. **Reproach of darkness:** These are curses, enchantments and parental dedications. **Joshua 5:9** the Lord said unto Joshua ***"this day I have rolled away the reproach of Egypt from off you"*** Remember, Joshua did not go by himself to Egypt, his ancestors went to live in Egypt. But, he was subjected to the captivity and the attack of the Egyptians. Whatsoever the enemies have covenanted with your ancestors, that is now working against your life, shall be

scattered by the Blood of Jesus Christ. When Jesus was on the cross and Pontius Pilate washed his hand he said 'I will not be part of the blood of this innocent man.' But, the crowd that was gathered made this shocking declaration ***"let his blood be upon us and upon our children."*** Any curse that your parents or ancestors have covenanted themselves into, that is now working against your life, shall break by fire. The agreement of your fathers to idols and their dedications against your life shall be utterly destroyed.

4. **Dreams Relating to the Feet:** The enemy attacks the spirit of man in their dreams. They subject people to confusions and relocate them backwards; to their former houses in times of poverty, former schools or past regrettable positions. It is written "I will bring you back from where the enemy has driven you." The enemy spiritually connects people to negative places in other to demote their destinies. But the word of God that changes times and seasons will restore and relocate you to glory. Some people see themselves in the forest in the dream but they are not hunters. What are they doing at the forest in the dream? I pray that wherever the enemy has located your legs spiritually in other to work against your destiny; God will arise in His mercy and deliver you speedily in Jesus name. Amen.

The Dreams That Walk Against Your Feet

1. Falling from heights or someone beating you in the dream; unknown person or masquerade pursuing you in the dream. They send the spirit of fear and discouragement to people. The pursuer may catch them and mercilessly beat them till they wake up.
2. Descending from stairs in a dream: You see yourself in a duplex and you are walking down the stairs. It is an evil dream that works to demote your destiny.
3. Missing road in the dream: Some people will be going somewhere in the dream but all of a sudden, they do not know the road again. It is the power that wants to plant confusion against your movement.

4. Some people in the dream see a person standing on one leg cursing them; the other leg shall be cut to pieces in the name of Jesus Christ.
5. At times they see themselves in a vehicle and unknown person will be driving them. Any power trying to manipulate or teleguide your life shall be scattered by fire.
6. Some people in the dream would be walking to somewhere but at a point, they try to move but their legs would be very heavy. Something is hindering their promotion.
7. To some people in their dream, the enemy will push them into a pit. Any power pushing your life into destruction shall die by fire. The power that capture your feet in other to bury you shall be destroyed for your sake in Jesus name.

When the enemy rose against the good works of God in the lives of Paul and Silas (Acts 16:24-26). They gave instructions to jailer to bind their feet. Bible says that their feet were tied to stocks. But, when they began to pray, the earthquake of deliverance manifested in the prison. The foundation of the prison was shaken; the doors where open and everyone's bands were loosed. Every invisible chain that is tying down your feet shall break by the power of God.

Malachi 4:3 "And you shall tread down the lawless and wicked, for they shall be ashes under the soles of your feet in the day that I shall do this, says the Lord of hosts." The power of God on your feet will command dry bones to come alive in vital areas of your life. Your dead businesses, marriages and prayer life will resurrect by fire. ***Ezekiel 37:10 "So I prophesied as He commanded me, and breath came into them, and they lived, and stood upon their feet, an exceedingly great army."*** Your gifts and talents will begin to manifest profits for you; and your denied benefits will be restored. We walk in abundant favour because our feet are blessed. Your feet must reject the shoe of your fathers; it must also reject the pit of darkness in your father's house. Powers of the grave assigned to arrest your feet shall be destroyed totally. Your feet will not take you to the place where the sun of glory will not shine on you.

The bible says "he that calls the name of Jehovah, give him no rest until he has made Jerusalem a praise in the earth." It means that if you know that your victory will come from God, continue to pray until your testimonies manifest and your life becomes a praise. ***Zephaniah 3:20 says "For I will give you fame and praise among all the peoples of the earth"***

STEPS TO MAINTAIN A CLEAN FEET

Joshua 14:9 "So Moses swore on that day, saying, 'Surely the land where your foot has trodden shall be your inheritance and your children's forever, because you have wholly followed the LORD my God." The scriptural method to maintain clean and healthy feet is by walking faithfully on the commandments of God. Spreading the Gospel of Jesus Christ and doing good to your neighbor will beautify your feet. You can also do physical washing of your feet with anointing oil, declaring the word of God to deliver your legs from plots of the wicked.

This is form of prayers on the feet, which I do regularly for myself, wife and children. I always command my feet to reject every instruction of darkness and walk steadily on the light of God.

It is good to pray regularly on the feet, speaking blessings, liberty and power of glorious possessions into your feet. We should always offer praises and thanksgiving to God; and be disciplined to keep our vows. Your feet must not run to evil, it defiles and pollutes the feet. Feet that stay in the light are those who stay in love, and the wisdom of God resonates in their lives.

I pray that the precious blood of our Lord Jesus Christ will wash your feet from every ancestral evil inheritance. We have redemption through the blood of Jesus Christ, the forgiveness of sins, in accordance with the riches of God's grace.

PRAYER POINTS

1. Evil bed prepared by the waster against my health, catch fire, burn to ashes in the name of Jesus Christ.
2. Wickedness of the wicked, assigned against my feet, die by fire, in Jesus name.

3. Idol powers that has captured my feet, release my feet and die, in Jesus name.
4. Sentence from courts of darkness against my family, I reject you, DIE, in Jesus name.
5. Every hand of the strongman upon my feet, wither by fire, in Jesus name.
6. Power of death, assigned against my feet, be destroyed by fire in Jesus name.
7. Dark serpent in my foundation on assignment against my feet, die by fire in the name of Jesus Christ.
8. Every arrow of failure, fired into my legs, backfire, backfire in Jesus name.
9. Any curse issued against my legs, BREAK by fire, in Jesus name.
10. Powers on assignment to bury my feet, you are a liar, catch fire and die in Jesus name.
11. Agenda of disappointment and regret, programmed against my feet, die in Jesus name.
12. Powers manipulating my feet from the covens, I am not your candidate, die in Jesus name.
13. Power of the grave, assigned against my feet, you are a liar, break and die in Jesus name.
14. Curses that worked against my father, resurfacing against my life, break in Jesus name.
15. Evil marks and yokes of darkness in my place of birth, release my feet, die in Jesus name.

CHAPTER FOUR

Privileges Of Crying Out To God

Crying is expression of strong emotions towards a situation. Humanity passes through circumstances and troubles that require urgent divine intervention. There are temptations that are on a killing mission and unless God intervenes the victim would die. When people are going through sufferings that deny their peace and joy of living, they cry to God to turn the situation around. We cry to God when we trust that only Him has the solution to our problems. By crying to God, we empty ourselves trusting in His mercies. Crying out to God is an act of desperation and total concentration. Some deep problems are adamant to prayers, until we cry to God for directions and instant deliverance. When crying to God, we fervently express our pains and faith in Him, as our kindhearted father. In all forms of communication with God, crying brings faster result. When the disciples prayed for an epileptic person but could not cure him; Jesus remarked ***"this kind does not go out except by prayer and fasting."*** Matthew 17:21. Deep problems require fervent and committed cry to God; this approach usually involves fasting with tenacity.

Psalm 34:17 "The righteous cry out and the Lord hears, and delivers them out of all their troubles." When a problem overwhelms a man he cries out to God, showing his total and unconditional surrender to the Almighty. A distressed soul is desperate for help, but there are no directions or hope of any solution until he cries to God. ***Psalm 18:6 "In my distress I called upon the Lord, and cried out to my God; He heard my voice from His temple, and my cry came before Him, even to His ears."*** When a problem is so severe and nothing humanly possible can be done, we must cry to God whose power knows no impossibility. When the Israelites could not find fresh water in the wilderness, ***"Moses cried out to the Lord, and the Lord showed him a tree. When he cast it into the waters, the waters were made sweet." (Exodus 15:25).***

For example, if seven patients are in a hospital ward and the doctor entered with files to examine them serially from number one to seven. But suddenly the person at number five, began to cry desperately with a loud shout "Doctor, doctor, I am dying, doctor please I need help." The doctor would jump the queue to attend to the crying patient. That is exactly what happens when we cry out to God. Crying, draws the host of heaven to give expeditious attention to our requests.

It brings urgent divine intervention to our situation. Crying makes God attend to our petition speedily. He treats our concerns with utmost urgency and interest. Jesus had to stop and gave urgent attention to the request of Blind Bartimaeus because he cried desperately and passionately. ***Mark 10:47-52 when blind Bartimaeus, heard that it was Jesus of Nazareth, he began to cry out and say, "Jesus, Son of David, have mercy on me!" Then many warned him to be quiet; but he cried out all the more, "Son of David, have mercy on me!" So Jesus stood still and commanded him to be called. And throwing aside his garment, he rose and came to Jesus. So Jesus answered and said to him, "What do you want Me to do for you?" The blind man said to Him, "Rabboni, that I may receive my sight." Then Jesus said to him, "Go your way; your faith has made you well." And immediately he received his sight and followed Jesus on the road.*** Your case becomes the utmost priority of God when you cry out in faith to him, with all your heart. Blind Bartimaeus refused to be stopped by the people around him, he cried yet the more ***"Jesus, son of David, have mercy on me."***

A person who is desperately in need of God's intervention can do anything possible to draw His attention. Those who make mention of the Lord's name should not keep silent, give Him no rest until you receive desired testimony. Effectual fervent prayer of the righteous person avails much.

Crying to God draws the presence and power of the highest to take over your circumstances. When we cry to God, He comes with the power of "Enough is Enough" to rebuke our enemies. Crying passionately to God is sincere expression of deep hatred for the unfavorable situation and seeking God to change it. You must hate your situation before you cry for change. Only those who hate their chains can cry for freedom. A cry for change must be with total determination and violence in the spirit.

Jabez cried to God to rewrite his family history. ***1 Chronicles 4:10 "And Jabez called on the God of Israel saying, "Oh, that You would bless me indeed, and enlarge my territory, that Your hand would be with me, and that You would keep me from evil, that I may not encounter pain!" So God granted him what he requested."***

God will fulfill the desire of them that fear him: He also will hear their cry and will save them.

You can cry against a situation and the power of God will cause the change. The principle of the gospel is that you should not cry bitterly or sorrowfully in defeat about a situation. Instead, you let out a violent cry to God to change the situation. The Bible teaches that we must not lament about a mountain, we must courageously cast the mountain away without doubt, and it will obey.

A child of God should not fear the enemy or worry in pains about any problem or mountains of impossibilities; you wage war in form of battle cry, using the weapons in God's armory to destroy the enemy. The just shall live by faith; and without faith, it is impossible to please God.

Jesus did not feel defeated when He heard about the death of Lazarus, He moved with faith; and prayed to God. ***Jesus cried with a loud voice, "Lazarus, come forth!" (John 11:43).***

The resurrection power of God manifested and Lazarus that was dead came back to life.

You can cry against your dead business, dead marriage or dead virtues and the resurrection power of the Lord Jesus Christ will inject the power of life into them. ***"Jesus offered up prayers and supplications with fervent cries and tears to Him who was able to save Him from death" (Hebrews 5:7).*** You can cry against evil judgments, witchcraft decisions, fear and sicknesses.

There are situations that seems confusing and hopeless but, when we cry to God, He will provide guidance. When Hagar was distraught, she lifted her voice and wept because her son was dying of thirst. God heard the cry and gave Hagar the solution. ***Genesis 21:19 "Then God opened her eyes, and she saw a well of water. And she went and filled the skin with water, and gave the lad a drink."*** Anytime God's people are thirty without hope of any visible water, He gives directions to provide the water. It means that in the midst of scarcity of blessings, we need to cry to God; He will provide the directions that will miraculously produce our desired blessings. Until you let out a fervent cry to the Almighty, some stubborn situations would not change. Crying requires dogged determination, tenacity and trust in God as the only source of help.

Your zealous and persistent cry will cause heaven to suspend every other matter and give priority to you. Crying requires courage and refusal to accept the negative. When you challenge an unrepentant enemy with a consistent and passionate cry to God, the enemy must bow. Violent cry in prayers will release the finger of God to interrupt the operation of darkness. It announces the supremacy of the Lord of Host, as Jehovah the God of all flesh; with whom all things are possible. The fastest method to divine direction in hopeless situations is holy cry to God.

When the children of Israel camped in Rephidim, and there was no water for the people to drink; they thirsted there for water, and the people complained against Moses, and said, "Why is it you have brought us up out of Egypt, to kill us and our children and our livestock with thirst?" ***Exodus 17:4-6 So Moses cried out to the Lord, saying, "What shall I do with this people? They are almost ready to stone me!" And the Lord said to Moses, "Go on before the people, and take with you some of the elders of Israel. Also take in your hand your rod with which you struck the river, and go. Behold, I will stand before you there on the rock in Horeb; and you shall strike the rock, and water will come out of it, that the people may drink."*** The power of God miraculously produced water from the rock. This is blessing from unexpected source.

It proves that when God hears your cry, he can command your haters, naysayers and even those who had earlier rejected you, to go out of their ways to bless you. When situation seems unbearable and your helpers have deserted you, cry to God. When your family are going through circumstances that defy human solutions, or your business encounters unexpected difficulties; it is time to cry to God who changes times and seasons. The God of might and majesty, whose presence melts every mountain of impossibility will arise and turn your scarcity to abundance.

Some time ago, a young man came to me for urgent prayers. He received a disturbing call from his brother at the hospital, saying that he may not survive the sickness. He was so scared that his brother may not come out of the hospital alive. I told him that "we should cry unto God, to release His Healing power that never fails." I encouraged him with the scriptures that says "The Sun of righteousness shall arise with healing in His wings" and that power of God is still moving about to heal the sick. I further assured him that Jesus, the great physician, will visit his brother with power of His goodness. I held hands with him and we prayed fervently, crying unto God.

I raised several prayer points that addressed the foundation, declaring that vulture of his father's house shall not feed on the carcass of his destiny. It was already evening and we could not go to the hospital until the next day. But I remember telling the man to settle it in his mind that "before we get to the hospital tomorrow morning, your brother's story will change." He said "amen" but he was still uneasy and fearful.

As early as 8:00am the next morning, he came for me to follow him to the hospital which was about two hours' drive. Surprisingly, when we got to the hospital and waited at the reception, the sick brother came to meet us, feeling very strong and happy. We were all surprised by the miracle working power of the Almighty God. The sick brother who was talking about death the previous day, told us that "he is now healthy." Though he did not know that we already cried to God concerning his situation. Bible says "call unto God on the day of trouble, He will deliver you and you will glorify Him." Whoever calls on the name of the Lord shall be saved.

When the children of Israel cried against the wall of Jericho, it fell down flat. It is not in vain that the Bible says "on the day I cry unto the Lord, then shall my enemies turn back, this I know for the Lord is with me." Your enemy may be the problems in your marriage, it could be obstacles in your investments, it can also be oppositions to your next level. I declare that whatever is saying no to your testimonies shall fall down and die by fire in Jesus name.

Few years ago, a young boy that attended my prayer center, called very early in the morning that I should quickly come to their house to pray for his mother. When I got there, the father was already crying and the whole house was in disarray. "What happened?" I asked. The mother drank bottle of beer in the dream and woke up without being able to speak or hear.

I prayed for her, and the Lord told me that the woman would hear and talk that day. The husband was very anxious, stressed and shaking. He tried to explain several things about their family but I kept assuring him that God has intervened in his wife's situation. Immediately after extensive fervent prayers, calling on the name of the Lord Jesus Christ, the woman's situation began to amend gradually. She was moving her mouth but her words were not audible yet. I went out for a program and told them to stop crying and start glorifying God for answering our prayers.

At exactly 4:00pm that day, the young boy called me with great jubilations on the phone, and I spoke with all the family members' one after the other. I discussed with the same woman that was deaf and dumb. She was speaking fluently and discussing perfectly; and we glorified God together. The mystery of crying to God is absolute concentration and focus on God alone. You must surrender everything to God, seeking him with all your heart. God hears the cry of the humble and deliver them from trouble. Crying is the best spiritual activity that releases undiluted information from the Holy Spirit unto us. It opens our spiritual eyes to see the wonders of God. Crying to God is declaring that the enemy shall not have the final say concerning our situation. It is total reliance on the deliverance power of the Highest; proclaiming that agenda of darkness shall be overturned. We cry to enforce the victory won by the Lord Jesus Christ on the cross at Calvary, which empowers the believer to overcome all unfavorable circumstances. ***Psalm 37:19 "They shall not be ashamed in the evil time, and in the days of famine they shall be satisfied".*** Whatever consumes or afflicts others shall not afflict us, because we are divinely sought-out by the mercy of God. To effectively cry for urgent answer from heaven, you must have deep knowledge of the word of God as your basis to release the miracle working power of God.

REASONS TO CRY TO GOD.

As Christians, we should appropriate the gospel of Christ into our lives and destinies. Apostle Paul said that "Kingdom of God is not in word but in power". We can only enjoy relationship with God when we understand the best ways to apply scriptural principles to live in the supernatural. The word of God is the basis of everything we do as children of light. ***"This is the confidence that we have in God, that if we ask anything according to His will, He hears us."*** (1 John 5:14). First, our prayers must be according to His will. Jesus says "Thy will be done on earth as it is done in heaven". For you to effectively practice the method of crying to God, you must ensure that your desire is according to His will. We are created to perform the works of God and magnify His name to all nations of the earth. To achieve that, we must tap into the power of God, using it to defeat all unrighteousness and overthrow the enemy. The wicked is proud and unyielding but when they see the supernatural power of God in action, they bow by force. ***Daniel 3:24-25 Then King Nebuchadnezzar was astonished; and he rose in haste and spoke, saying to his counselors, "Did we not cast three men bound into the midst of the fire?" They answered and said to the king, "True, O king." 25 "Look!" he answered, "I see four men loose, walking in the midst of the fire; and they are not hurt, and the form of the fourth is like the Son of God."*** He commanded the three Hebrew children to come out of the midst of fire and declared that ***"there is no other God who can deliver like this"*** In verse 28, Nebuchadnezzar spoke, saying, ***"Blessed be the God of Shadrach, Meshach, and Abed-Nego, who sent His Angel and delivered His servants who trusted in Him."*** The power of God operating in you must shock your enemies, and end wicked activities for your sake. God will use you to advertise the greatness of His power and the enemies boasting against you, will be woefully disappointed.

After preaching in a particular Church some time ago; the resident Pastor requested that I pray for a man in his fifties who had severe medical condition. His ailment was terminal and he was afraid that he may die soon. When we entered the prayer room, he brought out some papers from hospital, so that I could see the seriousness of his sickness; but I told him that my business is the report of Jesus Christ, the Great Physician. I refused to see the medical reports because I did not want anything to cause hindrance on my faith. He was visibly feeling devastated and restless but, I quickly encouraged him on the power of God over all circumstances. Within few minutes, we went into high praises to God. Due to the fact that I did not bother to know the name of his terminal sickness, I resolved that God will reveal the right prayer points for the situation. We continued praising and thanking God for more than thirty minutes before I heard one prayer point very clearly. I told him to cry seriously to God in the prayer which says "Jesus, son of David, have mercy on me." We said the prayer for about one hour and God open my eyes showing "three days". Then, I stopped him and we started thanking God for answering the prayer. I told him to go to hospital for medical test again in three days' time and show the result to the Pastor. The Spirit of God had assured me that his problem is over. The following Sunday, I came to the same Church and he gave testimony in the presence of the congregation.

After the Church service on that Sunday, he started thanking me profusely; saying "Pastor, you have saved my life, you don't know what you have done for me" but I told him that the healer is Jesus Christ, and that I am only a vessel used by God. We excitedly glorified God together.

God hears the cry of His children. The finger of God shall nullify every negative report concluded against your life, and you will have joy and gladness. I pray that the great physician, Jesus Christ, will manifest His healing power upon your life and family in Jesus name. Amen.

Sometimes, bad things happen to good people. You may have consistently feared God and maintained a righteous living. But surprisingly, unexpected problems begin to threaten your existence. The plan of darkness could begin to raise its ugly head against your life. The enemy had conspired to cause you shame and there is no way out. The wicked from unexpected quarters decides to frame you up, they gather satanic evidences to frustrate and ridicule your reputation.

You need to cry unto God when the storms of life are raging; do not surrender to adversity.

King Asa did what was good and right in the eyes of the Lord his God. But the Ethiopian army rose up against him with wicked determination to destroy his kingdom. It was neither his fault nor sin from him that cause the trouble. Bible says ***"many are the afflictions of the righteous."***

So, he understood that righteousness and carefulness may not insulate him completely from the troubles of life. ***2 Chronicles 14:11 "And Asa cried out to the Lord his God, and said, "Lord, it is nothing for You to help, whether with many or with those who have no power; help us, O Lord our God, for we rest on You, and in Your name we go against this multitude. O Lord, You are our God; do not let man prevail against You!"*** He released a heart cry that pierced the heaven straight to the Throne of God. He exercised profound faith resting on God's goodness and took action. The Lord heard his cry and smote the Ethiopians before Judah, and soundly defeated them to the extent that Ethiopians did not try to fight against Israel for another 300 years.

When believers cry out to the Lord in their trouble, He brings them out of their distresses. God attends to desire of the righteous who trembles at His word. He will hear your cry and destroy the plans of the wicked fashioned against your family.

By crying to God, we offer direct and precise prayers to Him. The distractions of the world which includes movies, music, platitudes, social media hypes and unpalatable breaking news; can make your regular prayers too shallow on daily basis. However, there is a kind of prayer that undermines the happenings of the world, it come from the heart that totally seeks intervention of God. Heal me or I die, deliver me or I perish, oppressions must end, my enemies will not write the last chapter of my life-these are prayers from depth of the heart.

You need to cry out in prayers for God to open your spiritual eyes to His purposes for your life.

The enemy of our soul shrinks and crumbles when our heart aligns with the Spirit of God, so he does everything possible to distract and dissuade us. You need to know the will of God concerning vital areas of your life-investments, marriage, contracts and visions for your life.

WHEN SHOULD WE CRY TO GOD.

1. When the strong enemy has concluded plans to sink your destiny. ***Psalm 18:17 "He sent from above, He took me; He drew me out of many waters. He delivered me from my strong enemy, from those who hated me, for they were too strong for me. They confronted me in the day of my calamity, but the Lord was my support".*** There are moments in a person's life that the enemy says "it is over". The agenda of the wicked had worked for them, and they had taken you unawares. In fact, there is no possible way of escape for you, and the enemies are already beginning to mock you. ***Job 20:5 "The triumphing of the wicked is short and joy of the hypocrite is just for a moment."*** The good news is that the wicked shall not have the last laugh concerning our destinies. During such trying period, some trusted friends would disappoint you. All possible avenues of solution had failed; and the soul melts because of trouble. There are troubles that draw people to the gates of death; their soul abhorred all manner of food, the heart is confused and depressed. The devil in his wickedness would trigger destructive imaginations, thoughts and nightmares that would further devastate the person. Bible says ***"They reel to and fro, and stagger like a drunken man, and are at their wits' end."*** **Psalm 107:27**

   When stubborn situation gets to such level of despair, the best solution is cry out to the Lord.

   Psalm 107:28 "Then they cry out to the Lord in their trouble, and He brings them out of their distresses. He calms the storm, so that its waves are still. Then they are glad because they are quiet; so He guides them to their desired haven." Our God is a man of war; the Lord is His name. When you cry to God in the midst of all the troubles, He appears to turn the table against the enemy. He manifests to break the gates of bronze, and cut the bars of iron asunder. The same enemy that struggles to see your end will perish in their evil pit. It is time to cry out to the Lord with all our hearts. This is the best way to prepare for the strong finish. ***"When the captains of the chariots saw Jehoshaphat,***

that they said, it is the king of Israel. Therefore, they compassed about him to fight: but Jehoshaphat cried out, and the Lord helped him; and God moved them to depart from him" (2 Chronicles 18:31). God delivered him from midst of killers.

2. Necessity of Directions from God: There are times that all we need to be saved is direction from God. When Pharaoh drew near, the children of Israel lifted their eyes, and behold, the Egyptians marched after them. So they were very afraid, and the children of Israel cried out to the Lord. Moses was instructed by the Lord saying ***"Tell the children of Israel to go forward. But lift up your rod, and stretch out your hand over the sea and divide it. And the children of Israel shall go on dry ground through the midst of the sea" (Exodus 14:15-16).*** Moses was told the role that he would play in order to achieve the final deliverance from Pharaoh. Your cry to God at critical times will open your eyes to the action that you must take, for desired miracle to appear. When you receive directions from God, He works with you to destroy the siege of the oppressor. You must cry against the Pharoah of your father's house; powers that troubled your parents and are now opposing your destiny. Crying is from the deepest of your heart, earnestly seeking for God to manifest His presence. The effective, fervent prayer of the righteous produces astounding results. Cry to deliver yourself and family from ancestral covenants and dark cycles***. Isaiah 45:11 Thus says the Lord, The Holy One of Israel "Ask Me of things to come concerning My sons; and concerning the work of My hands, you command Me."*** Trust in the Lord with all thine heart; and lean not unto thine own understanding. In all thy ways acknowledge him, and he shall direct thy paths.

Our God makes impossibility to be possible. When God direct your steps; safety and success are absolutely guaranteed. A day of passionate cry to God, can change your story from hopeless situation to overwhelming testimony. You need to cry for change! Every negative situation must change when children of God decides to cry to the heavenly father. You must cry for the Will of God to be done in your life as it is done in heaven. The peace of God will reign in your marriage, the joy of the Lord must overwhelm your business and the glory of God shall fill the temple of your destiny.

A CRY FOR CHANGE

Some years ago, a relative of mine had serious fire accident to the extent that the body was severely burnt; and she was rushed to the Hospital. One night, she was telling the senior sister who was with her at the hospital ward, that a woman was pushing her down from the bed. The sister said to her "there is no woman beside you." But she continued shouting that a woman was pushing her down. Within few minutes she started pleading with the sister to bring her up to the bed that the woman had pushed her down. But she was still on top of the bed physically, but invisible powers had relocated her to the ground, spiritually. The next day, the doctors said that she needed blood transfusion as the blood level in her body had become too low. Blood was donated for her that morning, and we felt that she was going to be alright. Surprisingly, at exactly 1:00am at night, we received call from the hospital that she was shouting that she could not breathe; she was gasping for breath. We quickly drove to the hospital which was only five minutes away. On getting there, I saw the attendant trying to put oxygen on her. I told the hospital attendant to allow me pray for her, that she will start breathing normally after my prayers. The attendant did not even listen to me, so I stepped aside and started crying to the Lord who delivers from the gate of the grave. About ten minutes into the prayers, she called me to come closer, and pleaded with me to pray like this "any naked young man pursuing me with cutlass, fall down and die." As I was crying to God for intervention, I was also crying against the naked young man in the spirit realm, on assignment to cut short her destiny. Within twenty minutes into the prayers, the Oxygen stopped working and the attendant came to fix it, but I stopped him.

I requested that the Doctor should check her first. Fortunately, the doctor obliged, checked her and confirmed that she had started breathing properly. God heard my cry and delivered her from death. I was confident that my cry to God would not go unnoticed. The Lord whom we seek will suddenly appear to overturn our troubles. Bible says "When I cry out to the Lord, then my enemies will turn back; this I know, because God is for me." My prayer on that night at the hospital was not gentleman prayer. It was desperate cry to the Lord who is able to deliver from the violence of the fire, and from the mouth of the lion. You must cry to avert the desire of the wicked fashioned against your life. When confronted by strong enemy, cry to God for deliverance. The devil will not waste your destiny and you will not die before your time.

The children of Israel wept in despair because of the bondage in Egypt, and they cried out; and their cry came up to God. So God remembered His covenant with their fathers and decided to deliver them. ***Exodus 3:7 And the Lord said to Moses: "I have surely seen the oppression of My people who are in Egypt, and have heard their cry because of their taskmasters, for I know their sorrows. So I have come down to deliver them out of the hand of the Egyptians"***

Taskmasters were subjecting the children of Israel to sorrows, severe bondage and afflictions but when they cried unto the Lord, He sent Moses to deliver them. When you cry unto God, He will remember his covenant upon your destiny, and plague your oppressors. Your cry to God will turn the table against your enemies. God will deflate the confidence of your adversaries and turn-away your captivity. Heaven will delegate helpers to deliver you from stubborn adversaries.

Anytime heaven decides to attend to any matter, the stronghold of the oppressor must be demolished. The Lord will enforce expiry date upon your sorrows; and your weakness will receive the strength of God.

During the storm on the Sea of Galilee, the disciples acknowledged Jesus' power to rescue them. They cried out to Jesus saying, ***"Lord, save us! We are perishing!" (Matthew 8:25).*** Then, Jesus arose and rebuked the winds and the sea, and there was a great calm. The waves of oppression will not overtake the boat of your destiny. The same Jesus will attend to your cry and arise to defend you from the storms of life. You need to cry out like the disciples to get attention of Jesus. When Apostle Peter walked out on the water at the invitation of Jesus, he was afraid; and beginning to sink he cried out, saying, "Lord, save me!" Immediately, Jesus stretched out His hand and caught him" (Matthew 14:30–31). It is interesting to note that God answers speedily anytime we cry out to Him. We are further assured that no matter how far the enemy had travelled against our destiny, the intervention of God will terminate their efforts. This also proves that we should not be afraid of the enemy because we have the Almighty God on our side.

The effectiveness of crying to God also confirms the scriptural declaration which says ***"For this purpose the Son of God was manifested, that He might destroy the works of darkness"***

The pit was not the end of Joseph, the prison did not end the ministry of Paul and Silas, lion's den was not the end of Daniel, and the furnace of fire was not the end of Shadrach, Meshach and Abed-Nego. Definitely, the works of the enemy will not terminate your destiny in Jesus name.

Some people go through series of unexpected failures at the edge of breakthroughs. They are related to men of caliber that had abundant capacity to help them, but none is ready to help. There are people that evil pattern in the family line is limiting them from attaining the next level.

There can be five women in a family and all of them encounter bitter experiences in their respective marriages. Some families have up to five graduates but none of them is doing well. The bible revealed that **"evil horns can be in a family to scatter their efforts, so that no one could lift up his head" Zechariah 1:21** You need to cry to the Lord in violent anger to kill the serpent of darkness in your foundation. Call down the fire of God to roast any foundational power calling for your demotion. ***"If you can boldly say to the mountain, be thou removed and be cast into the sea, without any doubt in your mind, it shall be so" (Matthew 11:23).***

You must confront and reject any mountain opposing your advancement. Righteousness of God is essentially to destroy the oppression of darkness for God's will to reign in our lives. God will hear your cry and commandeer helpers for you. ***Judges 3:15 "But when the children of Israel cried out to the Lord, the Lord raised up a deliverer for them: Ehud the son of Gera, the Benjamite, a left-handed man."*** The Lord knows the best way to deliver His people out of troubles. When you passionately cry unto God, He will answer and show you great and mighty things, which you knew not.

THINGS TO REQUEST WHEN CRYING TO GOD

Holy Bible advises that "we should open our mouth wide and God will fill it." Our good shepherd is able to release great blessings unto His children. There must be a specific request in our heart when crying to God. When Prophet Elijah told his servant Elisha to ask for one thing, he said "I pray thee, let a double portion of thy anointing be upon me." Persistent cry to God will make heaven to open a blank cheque for you. Therefore, you must ask for something great that will be permanent settlement in your life. King Solomon asked God for Wisdom because he knew that wisdom is greater than money. A cry flows from a desperate heart that has come to the realization that only God can save, deliver and supply our needs.

God will fulfill the desire of them that fear him: he also will hear their cry, and will save them.

We must pray for God's intervention in the affairs of our families and nations at large.

We should also pray for the Lord to raise and position the right leaders in our public offices.

Let us be quick to cry out to Him with humility, sincerity, and faith. The earth is the Lord's and the fullness thereof; He is the creator and possessor of the heavens and the earth.

PRAY FOR YOUR HELPERS: A young man came to me for prayers, saying that his problem is that anytime someone promises to help him, the person would encounter troubles that will make it impossible to fulfill the promise. He concluded that a particular power was attacking his helpers in order to keep him in perpetual poverty. I told him that there are two steps to solve the problem. Firstly, he must develop severe hatred against that power opposing the goodness of God in his life. ***David said "I hate them that hate the Lord, I hate them with perfect hatred"*** Secondly, he will cry deeply from the heart against the enemy of God's glory in his life. With that hatred from the heart, you will cry against the activities of that power going before you to attack your helpers. I joined him in serious prayers that day, crying to God to remove the stronghold of darkness creating problem for his helpers. Thank God, his ways opened and he started recording testimonies after our prayers. There are stubborn pursuers that will not turn back unless and until you fervently cry unto God. There are strong enemies whose duty is to attack and frustrate anyone who decides to help you. They want you to remain in the wilderness of life, as hewer of wood or drawer of water.

Elijah cried out, and God revived a dead child of the widow who was helping him.

I Kings 17:20–22 "Then he cried out to the Lord and said, "O Lord my God, have You also brought tragedy on the widow with whom I lodge, by killing her son?" 21 And he stretched himself out on the child three times, and cried out to the Lord and said, "O Lord my God, I pray, let this child's soul come back to him." 22 Then the Lord heard the voice of Elijah; and the soul of the child came back to him, and he revived."

The enemy had killed the child of same widow helping Elijah, but he cried to God and the helper's child came back to life. Any power on assignment to kill your helper in order to impoverish your life, that power shall receive the stone of fire and die the death of Goliath.

There are people whose suffering started on the day their helper died. If the oppressor sees the date that you will meet a helper who will bless you abundantly, they can go before the date to kill the helper or cause problems against the person, that will make him unable to help you. I pray that any agenda of darkness against the helpers of your destiny shall perish by fire in Jesus name.

Holy Cry to God for Fruit of the Womb has become the most challenging battle of women in their marriages. The enemy may not stop a woman from getting the right partner for marriage, but may struggle to stop her from having children at the right time. The problem of child bearing have caused women so much pains, distractions, heartaches and wastage in their marriages.

The fruit of the womb is one of the most essential reasons for getting married. Hannah poured out her soul before the Lord. ***1 Samuel 1:10-11 "And she was in bitterness of soul, and prayed to the Lord and wept in anguish. Then she made a vow and said, "O Lord of hosts, if You will indeed look on the affliction of Your maidservant and remember me,***

and not forget Your maidservant, but will give Your maidservant a male child, then I will give him to the Lord all the days of his life, and no razor shall come upon his head."

You can cry to God for the fruit of the womb because good children can only come from God. Psalmist prayed "Deliver me from strange children; that our sons may be as plants grown up in their youth; that our daughters may be as pillars, sculptured in palace style"

I pray that God will bless your marriage with children that will profit your destiny in Jesus name.

APOSTLE PAUL CRIED OUT TO GOD FOR DELIVERANCE:

There are powers that attack people at the edge of their breakthroughs; they prepare to turn a person's day of joy into sorrow. They push people to disastrous mistake at the most crucial step to success. These are spiritual embargos and evil gates resisting your star from shinning. They position wicked agents who would adamantly take irrational actions that will frustrate your rightly deserved results. ***2 Corinthians 12:7 "And lest I should be exalted above measure through the abundance of the revelations, there was given to me a thorn in the flesh, the messenger of Satan to buffet me, lest I should be exalted above measure. For this thing I besought the Lord thrice, that it might depart from me. And he said unto me, My grace is sufficient for thee: for my strength is made perfect in weakness. Most gladly therefore will I rather glory in my infirmities, that the power of Christ may rest upon me."*** The enemy became aware of Paul's vision of greatness and it wickedly attached a demoting spirit to hinder him.

You need to cry out to God to remove the strongman of wickedness opposing the lifting up of your head. It is necessary to accept the inconvenience of staying awake and hold night vigils.

As you cry earnestly with fasting and prayers, the messenger of satan assigned against your promotion shall hear the rebuke of the Lord, and flee away by fire. God will rebuke the wicked! "At Your rebuke, O God of Jacob, both the chariot and horse were cast into a dead sleep."

Our Lord Jesus Christ advised that we must be consistent and tenacious in our prayers until result comes. Luke 18:1 "men ought always to pray and not to faint." God brings about justice for His elect who cry to Him day and night, without any delay. Our help only comes from the Lord who made the heavens and the earth, the creator of the ancient hills. God wants us to cry out to Him with our needs. ***I rise before the dawning of the morning, and cry for help; I hope in Your word. Psalm 119:147.*** I enjoin you to cry earnestly like Zerubbabel against any obstacle, disability or mountain confronting your progress. ***Zechariah 4:7 "Who are you, O Great Mountain? Before Zerubbabel you shall become a plain!" And he shall bring forth the capstone with shouts of "Grace, grace to it!".*** You too can shout this life-changing cry: "Who art thou great mountain before (Felix Nkadi) thou shall become plain in Jesus name.

PRAYER POINT

1. Inherited battles in my life, I cry against you, die by fire in the name of Jesus Christ.
2. Powers that troubled my parents and are now troubling me, die forever in Jesus name.
3. Agenda of wasters, fashioned against my destiny, scatter by fire in Jesus name.
4. Arrows of darkness fired against my star, go back to your senders in Jesus name.
5. Serpent in my foundation, swallowing my testimonies, catch fire, die, in Jesus name.
6. Witchcraft decision against the glory of my destiny, expire by fire in Jesus name.
7. Dark manipulations in my dream, assigned to demote my destiny, die in Jesus name.
8. Pharaoh of my father's house, assigned to pursue me into the red sea, die in Jesus name.
9. Every base of the enemy inviting me to demotion, scatter by fire in the name of Jesus.
10. Flying wickedness in my heaven, fall down and die in the name of Jesus.

11. Every satanic decision taken against my progress be nullified in the name of Jesus.
12. Every power of darkness, that has arrested my ministry and calling, release me now, in the name of Jesus Christ.
13. Every power of darkness, following me about, die by fire, in the name of Jesus.
14. Oh Lord, remove the penalty of judgment upon my life and calling, in Jesus name.
15. Every satanic weapon formed against my destiny, backfire, in the name of Jesus.

CHAPTER FIVE

Divine Helpers For Glorious Destiny

The greatest need of all creatures is divine settlement. As the word of God is settled in Heaven, the help of God settles all the struggles and needs of humanity. The Help of God is the secret behind every shining destiny. Every blessing and accomplishment on earth is as a result of help from God. ***Deuteronomy 33:26 "who is like unto the God of Jeshurun, who rides upon the heavens to help us."*** To make remarkable achievements in the journey of life, you need the help of God. A woman cried out to king of Israel saying, ***"Help, my lord, O king!" And he said, "If the Lord does not help you, where can I find help for you? (2 Kings 6:26-27).*** God is the ultimate source of help. The greatest force in the universe is divine intervention. The bible says that God changes times and seasons. When God appears in the midst of your fire, He neutralizes the effects and turn-away the heat from you. Help from God is the solution to all problems. God's intervention will change the equation of the enemy. Those who know the Lord and understand the power of His resurrection depends on divine help for exploits.

The greatest and most reliable therapy that brings the best solution to all problems; whether in your marriage, finance, or ministry is help from God. After creation, God identified a problem in Adam. He said, I will give you a helper. It means that God is the source and giver of help for humanity. ***Psalms 121:1 "I will lift my eyes unto the hills from whence cometh my help, my help come from the Lord who made the heaven and the earth."*** The originator and provider of help is God Himself. God is ever willing, able and ready to help us. In Exodus 18:4, after Moses gave birth to his son, he named him Eliazar and said ***"The God of my father was my help, and delivered me from the sword of Pharaoh."*** The same God will deliver you from strong enemies and lead you safely to your promised land. God delivers from gates of the grave, edge of the sword, mouth of the lions and from violence of fire. With God all things are possible. He knows the best way to deliver us out of every temptation.

The Bible says "I will deliver you from your struggles" I pray that anything that is making you to sweat without profits will be removed from your life, and you will begin to make sweat-less breakthroughs. God will make ways for you where there is no way. He will connect you to special helpers of your destiny. ***Psalm 124:8 says, "Our help is in the name of the Lord, Who made heaven and earth."*** When God is helping you, the arm of the wicked will be paralyzed for your sake; He will frustrate the best effort of your enemies. True help emanates from God. Most times, God uses men as machinery to help us. Some people are divinely and strategically positioned to help you achieve your goal. When God decides that somebody will be helped magnificently, He will commandeer men to perform the help. Between the day you were born and the day you die, you need a destiny helper. There is no man that can produce a baby alone, no matter how powerful he is. The power blocking your destiny helpers shall die.

The help of God will clothe your destiny, decorate your efforts and fortify you with required capacity to fulfill your goal. God will stop all powers that are hindering and distracting your helpers. Hand of the Lord God of Elijah shall draw the right persons to help and support you.

Our merciful God releases His powerful fingers to perform supernatural help to deliver His people. When God told Aaron to strike the dust with his rod to produce lice, the magicians of Pharaoh tried to imitate the signs but they failed, so they declared to Pharaoh that ***"this is the Finger of God."*** When God releases his finger into your situation, the best effort of the enemy will end in painful failure. The finger of God will destroy enchantments and break every captivity of darkness limiting your advancements. ***Jesus says "But if I cast out demons with the Finger of God, surely the Kingdom of God has come upon you."*** It means that the finger of God terminates every oppression of the devil and establishes His presence in our lives.

REASONS WHY WE NEED HELP FROM GOD

We need help from God because the challenges and burdens of life are too heavy for one to bear alone. ***"Cast your burden on the Lord and He shall sustain you-Psalms 55:22"*** The same God that showed up for Daniel and stopped the mouth of the lions will show up for you.

God will intervene to shut the mouth of any roaring lion on assignment to devour your destiny. The help of God is freely given to humanity. ***Romans 8:32 "He that spared not his own Son, but delivered Him up for us all, how shall He not with Him freely give us all thing?"***

The Help of God is free, but some human being will help you to enslave you. They desire to subject you to unholy tribute. The help from man are sometimes with selfish intentions to enslave and subjugate your life. They want to determine your steps and decide your destiny. You will receive the special help of God and He will make you a channel of blessings to others.

Divine Helpers that you must pray to receive.

1. **Good Brothers and Sisters:** One of the greatest blessing is good siblings. A good brother or sister will not forsake you in hard times. Your sibling in position of authority will promote and create opportunities that will advance your destiny. When God decides to promote a family, He starts with one person who will help others in need. The promotion of your good brother or sister will open doors of opportunities that will actualize your dreams. When the mercy of God visits a family of seven for example, it comes to one person who would generously spread the blessing to others. When Andrew met Jesus Christ, he first called his own brother Simon, and said to him, **"We have found the Messiah."** And he brought him to Jesus. A person whose brother is the governor of a State or President of the country, will definitely be sure of special favor in his career.

   When siblings in a family are united in love, they will watch each other's back and none will ever stand alone. As Abraham rescued Lot, and recovered his brother's goods that the enemy had carted away, your first human helper should be your own brother or sister. Do not forsake or disappoint your brothers in need. ***Genesis 14:14-16 "Now when Abram heard that his brother was taken captive, he armed his three hundred and eighteen trained servants who were born in his own house, and went in pursuit as far as Dan. 15 He divided his forces against them by night, and he and his servants attacked them and pursued them as far as Hobah, which is north of Damascus. So he brought back all the goods, and also brought back his brother Lot and his goods, as well as the women and the people."*** God helps and defend families who live in unity and love towards one another.

2. **PECULIAR ENEMIES:** These are unusual people that come across your life with evil intentions and strange actions, but the end will definitely benefit your destiny. At times, they oppress and oppose you but their ruthless actions do not discourage, distract or reduce you, rather it brings out the best in you. These are stubborn and unrepentant human beings that hate your existence. They are embittered by your progress; they hate to see good things around you. In fact, you did not do any wrong to them, but they desire to hurt, conspire, accuse, despise and ridicule you. These peculiar enemies bear false witnesses against you, without any fault of yours. They boast in their devilish ways and even threaten to terminate your life. But their wickedness will move you to depend solely on God. If there was no Goliath who opposed David and his people, David would not have become a wonder boy. If the brothers of Joseph did not try to terminate his destiny, he would not have gone to Egypt, let alone being a prime minister in foreign land.

   If strong enemies did not gather against Jehoshaphat, he would not have set his heart to seek the Lord, to the extent that he proclaimed a fast throughout all Judah. Activities of wicked enemies will draw you closer to God, and bring out hidden virtues to promote you.

   The Apostles prayed in Acts 4:29 "And now, Lord, behold their threatening: and grant unto thy servants, that with all

boldness they may speak thy word." Your uncle or the strong person in your office or profession, standing like Pharaoh against your advancement, can be the peculiar enemy that will bring out your hidden talents. That lion of darkness roaring to catch your flocks of greatness will manifest the David-like and Samson-like determination in you, to tear their mouths and recover your possessions. Your peculiar enemy can also be a confidant whom you erroneously trusted and had revealed deep personal secrets to him, but surprisingly the person is willing to destroy you.

The enemy in your life could be the helper for you, because your knowledge about their oppositions and betrayals will shape you to become a prayer warrior. These are enemies that bite without remnant. You know that if you fail to overcome them, they will finish you up. So, you must do everything possible to stop them before they kill you. The boastings and threats from Sennacherib strengthened Hezekiah's resolve to seek and trust God, the more. Some people would not have devoted much time to prayers and fasting, if not for stubborn enemies. The consciousness of your haters will encourage you to passionately take unusual spiritual steps. If you fail in the day of adversity your strength is small. So, you desire and resolve to expand your spiritual capacities both in prayers and study of the word of God, because you understand that certain powers are plotting your downfall.

Your awareness of the peculiar enemy will make you wake up in the night, denying yourself sleep in order to engage in warfare prayers. You will pray against conspiracies because of the strange enemies. The wickedness of your peculiar enemy will push you to abide firmly under the shadow of Almighty. God will go before you to scatter wicked associations gathered to waste your life. When God came to Joshua, He declared "this day, I will roll away every reproach of Egypt from off you" (Joshua 5:9). The reproach of the Goliath and Pharaoh of your father's house shall be rolled away. Every covenant of poverty that is working against your life shall be rolled away. Every door of affliction that the enemy has opened against you shall be closed by the blood of Jesus Christ. AMEN.

3. **The Exceptional spouse:** A person's marriage will either stabilize his destiny or destroy it. Your spouse will either make you a better person or a bitter person in life. Many great men have been reduced to nothing because of bad marriage. Your marital destiny is tied to the fulfillment of your goals in the land of the living. Samson lost his ordained powers and died prematurely because he loved the wrong woman. The enemy that wants to truncate your shining destiny begins by joining you to the wrong spouse. Your marriage determines your future generation and the devil is very interested about it. The Lord warned the children of Israel against mistakes in marriages. Marriage to wrong partner can destroy your faith in God, and attract his wrath against you. ***Deuteronomy 7:3-4 "You shall not make marriages with them. You shall not give your daughters to their sons, nor take their daughters for your sons. For they will turn your sons away from following Me."*** If you marry an enemy of God, the devil will be your in-law. The exceptional spouse will keep you focused on your essential purposes in life. They make you strive for excellence, and connect to things that will stabilize your destiny. They ensure that you create adequate time for the things of God. They will improve your prayer life and make sure that you grow spiritually. A person's wisdom can be measured by whom he chooses to be the life partner. Your spouse has a role to play to determine how your life will become. Adam was demoted from the garden of Eden because the devil entered his marriage. The person you marry will affect your relationship with God either positively or negatively.

The closest human being in your life is your spouse, and he or she occupies a very strategic position in your daily affairs. Nehemiah 4:14 advises that men should pray for their household, including their wives and children. It is very important that you always pray for your spouse and commit your marriage to the Lord Jesus Christ. Bible says ***"riches and wealth can be inherited but, good wife is from God."*** Your wife is the mother of your generation and must be in compliance with the purpose of God for your destiny. Beautiful destinies of some godly women have also been destroyed by wicked men. In fact, young men with sugar coated mouth have confused and devastated the virtues of many good girls.

4. **Ordained Promoters**: They are custodian of opportunities. They have the keys for your testimonies and turnaround breakthroughs. They have the mastery and the position to take you to highest level of glory. In fact, they are divinely empowered to deliver you from wicked agents on assignment to rubbish your destiny. Meeting them will close every gate of shame harassing your life. At times, I call them ordained king-makers because they have the spiritual ability to bring out the hidden royalty deposited in your life; which the enemy had struggled to bury. God uses them to relocate you to His glorious path for your destiny. One day, the butler, told Pharaoh about a young Hebrew boy he met in prison and pharaoh sent to call Joseph. That encounter promoted Joseph from prison to palace. Joseph was in prison until he met an ordained promoter in the person of Pharaoh, whom the Lord used to crown him a prime minister. Ordained promoters are story changing contacts, the day you meet them changes the narratives about your life. They are specially sent from the Lord.

   Meeting them will decorate and rebrand your life for good. The meeting is usually ordained from God, after serious prayers. A person may have searched for employment after years of graduating from University, a woman may have looked for good husband to marry but to no avail, a businessman may have desired a contract for long time, yet no hope; but after some targeted prayers, he or she meets someone who become worthy solution to the problems. They are divinely organized contacts that will promote your life; fruitful associations that will put an end to your sorrows. Then, your hidden gift would automatically appear and begin to shine. These promoters are heavenly vehicles with grace to fast track the fulfillment of your destiny. I pray that the Spirit of God will connect you to the ordained promoters in Jesus name.

5. **STRONG FRIEND**: They are special, patient and tolerant people in your life; they stay with you through thick and thin. These are people that genuinely identify greatness in your life and strengthen you to remain focus till you accomplish your purpose. There are

some people when they achieve breakthroughs or attain an enviable position, complacency and pride sets in, but if they have strong friends beside them, he will tell them about more goals to achieve. They see beyond your present status and believe that better days are ahead for you. These are dependable and available confidants who selflessly desire your growth and strengthens you in faith. They steadfastly encourage you that your present possession or position is just stepping stone to greater heights. Strong friends are not sycophants nor praise singers. They are humble and trusted people you can rely on in times of trouble. Jonathan was a strong friend to David, despite the fact that his father, King Saul wanted to kill David, yet he swore to protect David. Strong friends are honest and faithful; they do not mind who hates them for your sake. They are ready to bear any risk to ensure your safety. They sacrificially spend their resources to guarantee your safety and comfort.

They help to strengthen your weakness and complement your deficiencies. Strong friends are benevolent, faithful and always bold to look at your face and tell you the truth. They overlook your faults and correct you with love. Any time they notice mistakes in your actions; they quickly correct and never condemn you. They will not conspire, betray or take advantage of you. They become your strength in time of despair; at times, God uses them to deliver you from conspiracy. They are always reliable and available as good company to comfort you at all times. Anything you confide in them will remain a secret forever. They cannot be enticed with money or any juicy position to work against you. Jonathan loved David as he loved his own soul; strong friends love you from their heart.

6. **True Prophet of God**: ***Hosea 12:13 says "By a prophet, God brought Israel out of Egypt and by the hand of a prophet God preserved them"*** One day Elijah was troubled and frustrated to the extent that he asked God to kill him. But his solution started in 1st kings chapter 19 when God instructed him to anoint Hazeal to be prophet in Syria and anoint Elisha to be the prophet in his room. Everybody that is conscious of great destiny must have a room prophet. It does not mean that the prophet will be living

in the same house with you. But he is a true man of God who intercedes and stands in gap for you in prayers.

The bible says that God performs the counsel of His messengers, and establishes the word of His servants. Men of God are gifts in the body of Christ. They have severely sacrificed earthly comforts seeking power from God's presence; tarrying in fasting and prayers.

Bible says "Believe God, you will be established; believe his prophets and you shall prosper" Prophets are the mouth piece of the Almighty. When you encounter a true prophet of God, everything about you will change dramatically. In 1 Samuel chapter 9, Saul was looking for the horse of his father until he encountered Prophet Samuel, he became a king. ***Amos 3:7 "Surely, God will do nothing, until he reveals it to His servants, the prophets"***

Mark 4:11 Jesus told his disciples "unto you, it is given to know the mysteries of the Kingdom of God." You need a true prophet in your life for spiritual directions; he will teach you mysterious principles in the gospel of Christ. A young man was worried that his business was not moving well, surprisingly, a prophet called and gave him one prayer point which he prayed fervently, and from that moment, everything changed for good.

In Numbers chapter 12, God declared that Moses was a special prophet to Him, because Moses was faithful in all His house. Prophets have sacrificed so much to sustain themselves as temple of God. They have special rewards and receives extraordinary revelations from God. The bible says that ***"God has made his ministers flame of fire."*** The unrepentant enemy that is pursuing you will see them beside you spiritually, and their fire will pursue your enemy. Bible declares ***"Give water to a prophet in the name of a prophet you will receive the reward of a prophet."*** Prophets are oracles of God with authority to mandate performance of God's will in situations, and heaven establishes their declarations. God have special covenants with His prophets and He reveals secrets to them, concerning important matters. Solution to problems are revealed to His prophets to deliver the people.

7. **Jesus Christ.** The Lord is the greatest helper. Only wise men and women will seek Jesus Christ irrespective of their position, education or possession. Jesus Christ in our lives is the hope of Glory. He is the most important factor in the fulfillment of our destinies. Your relationship with Jesus Christ will equip you for supernatural possibilities, greater than your expectations. Jesus is the key to open heavens and manifestation of realistic testimonies. There are three major things that Jesus will do to help you. One is that he will give you peace. The bible calls Him the Prince of Peace. ***John 14:27 "Peace I leave with you, My peace I give to you; not as the world gives do I give to you. Let not your heart be troubled, neither let it be afraid."*** Jesus as your helper will deliver you from strong enemies and you will serve God without fear. He will deliver you from destructive choices and regrettable associations. He will always appear to defend his interest in our lives.

   Secondly, Jesus will lift you up. The bible says ***"God lifts a beggar out of the dunghill, He lifts a rich man from the dust"*** Jesus spoke to the man at the pool of Bathesda. ***"arise, take up your bed and walk."*** Therefore, meeting Jesus Christ as your helper will make you rise up from any valley, embargo or hindrance that is holding down your glory.

   Apostle Peter recognized the lifting up power of Jesus Christ, when he met the lame man at the beautiful gate, he said to him, ***"silver and gold have I none, but what I have I give unto you, in the name of Jesus Christ of Nazareth, rise up and walk".*** The same Jesus Christ is entering into your business; you will rise up and move forward. Jesus will enter into your family, you will rise up and prosper.

   Thirdly, He will comfort you. He said, ***"I will send you a comforter."*** He will give you the Spirit of wisdom and knowledge that will comfort your life. The spirit of God will lift up a standard against every flood of the enemy. God sent His word and healed His people and delivered them out of their destructions. The comforting power of Jesus Christ delivers you from every distress. Whether it is sicknesses or troubles from the enemy, God will deliver you to comfort you. ***Isaiah 49:13 "Sing, O heavens! Be***

> ***joyful, O earth! And break out in singing, O mountains! For the Lord has comforted His people, and will have mercy on His afflicted."*** I pray by the power of the word of God, any power that has taken it as a point of duty to distress your life, shall fall down and die in the name of Jesus.
>
> Every embargo of limitation that hinders members of your father's house, and is now limiting your life, that embargo shall scatter by fire in the name of Jesus Christ. Amen.

It is absolute fallacy when people say that God will only help those who help themselves. God can help you even when you cannot help yourself. The bible says that ***"God will deliver the needy when he cries, the poor also, and him who has no helper-Psalm 72:12"*** It is written that on the day I cried unto God, then shall my enemy turn back. As you cry to God, every enemy that has taken advantage of your destiny, shall receive the hail stone of fire and die. God will arise, and silence any witchcraft voice that is spoiling the mind of your helpers against you.

Isaiah 41:10 "Fear not for I am with thee, I am thy God I will strengthen you, I will help you." Men will deny you promotion but helpers of your destiny from God will locate and promote you. David said, happy is he that have the God of Jacob for his help, whose help is in the Lord His God. The help of God will make you to rejoice evermore, it will deliver you from sorrow, and catapult your life to greater heights. God said to Abraham, ***"I will bless you and make your name great and through you shall all the families of the earth be blessed."*** It means that divine help is perfect. God said he will perfect all that concerns us. Help from God is final settlement and its complete.

To secure help from above, you must receive Christ as your Lord and savior, and endeavor to identify His will for your life. As monkey cannot succeed inside water neither can a fish live on a tree, it is impossible for a person to prosper outside his divinely ordained habitat.

Total obedience to God is essential and inevitable criterion to attract divine help. If you are willing and obedient to God, you shall eat the good of the land. Those who obey and trust God will never be put to shame, no matter the volume of their enemies. Jehoshaphat knew that his human power may not withstand the armors of his enemies, so he sought the help of God with all his heart. And God answered him in ***2 Chronicles 20:17 "You will not need to fight in this battle. Position yourselves, stand still and see the salvation of the Lord, who is with you, O Judah and Jerusalem!' Do not fear or be dismayed; tomorrow go out against them, for the Lord is with you."*** On the day of the battle, Jehoshaphat, instead of putting the strongest armies with weapons to lead the way, he decided to set choir to sing praises to God without any physical weapon. Therefore, God performed great wonders in ***2 Chronicles 20:21-22 "And when he had consulted with the people, he appointed those who should sing to the Lord, and who should praise the beauty of holiness, as they went out before the army and were saying: "Praise the Lord, for His mercy endures forever." Now when they began to sing and to praise, the Lord set ambushes against the people of Ammon, Moab, and Mount Seir, who had come against Judah; and they were defeated."***

Blessed is the one who trusts in the Lord, whose confidence is in Him. To achieve great and indelible victories in life, you must seek the attention of God by all means. When there was a great storm of wind, and the waves beat into the ship so that it was now full; Jesus was in the hinder part of the ship, asleep on a pillow: but the Apostles woke him, saying, Master, do you not care that we perish? He arose, and rebuked the wind, and said unto the sea, "Peace be still." And the wind ceased, and there was a great calm. The help of God makes the ordinary to become the anointed. With God nothing shall be impossible, He sent angel with good news to virgin Mary, and she became the Mother of the savior of the whole world. God will merciful attend to your secret prayers and release the power of turn-around breakthroughs that will showcase His awesome glory in your life. It is written that ***"If you obey and serve God, you shall spend their days in prosperity, and your years in pleasures (Job 36:11)"***.

When He appeared after the death of Lazarus, he said **"I am the resurrection and life he that believeth in me though they be dead yet shall they live."** Jesus will visit your home, and any good thing that is dead in your life shall receive His resurrection power. Lazarus was not only taken back to life; he was also healed of the sickness that killed him. Bible says that God will surely perfect everything that concerns us. God will not only bless you financially, he will also make you a success in your marriage. The blessing of God will establish His health in your family. Jesus is the great physician. He will begin to balance everything about your life, and your present location shall not be your final destination. Any circumstance that is troubling your life and making you to cry secretly, God will appear and wipe away your secret tears, in the name of Jesus Christ.

PRAYER POINTS

1. I receive the anointing to become a star in my generation in Jesus name.
2. O Lord, breathe upon my destiny and change my story to glory in Jesus name.
3. I receive the anointing to sit on my throne of celebration in Jesus name.
4. Lord, give me divine direction that will propel my life to greatness, in the name of Jesus.
5. Every secret I need to know to excel spiritually and financially be revealed, in the name of Jesus Christ.
6. O Lord, give me the comforting authority to achieve effortless results in Jesus name
7. Lord, fill me with wisdom like an angel in the name of Jesus.
8. O God arise and guide me along the best pathway for my life in Jesus name.
9. Any power blocking the vision of God for my life, your time is up, die, in Jesus name.
10. Lord, give me power for maximum achievement in this place in the name of Jesus.
11. Lord, make my voice the voice of peace, deliverance, power and solution Jesus name.
12. O Lord, remove from me every form of distractions that has blocked my spiritual eyes and ears from visions and divine instructions concerning my life in Jesus name.

13. Oh Lord, anoint me to recover the wasted years in every area of my life, in Jesus name.
14. Garment of Pharaoh that is upon my life, be removed by fire, in the name of Jesus Christ.
15. My Father in heaven, arise in your mercy and use my life to showcase your glory in the name of Jesus Christ

CHAPTER SIX

The Importance Of Prayer Warfare

The efficacy of your salvation is the power of God that is deposited in you; and that power can only be sustained by the infilling of the Holy Spirit and persistent prayers. Prayer is the gateway to breakthroughs and dominion prosperity. It will strengthen your relationship with God and give you access to the presence of God. Your spiritual power is determined by your prayer life. Prayer is the deciding factor in every spiritual battle. The arm of God will always respond to violent prayers. **Psalm 65:2** ***"O God who hear prayers, unto You all flesh will come."*** God loves those who can fervently tarry at the altar of prayer. Consistent prayer will always bring everlasting power. Only prayerful Christians can effectively enjoy the power of God. When Jonah was in the belly of the fish, he prayed fervently and God commanded the fish to vomit him (Jonah 2:10). When there was prophecy of death against Hezekiah, he prayed earnestly and God sent the same prophet Isaiah to declare extension of life to him. Ephesians 6:18 advised that we should ***"Pray always with all prayer and supplication in the spirit."*** Prayer is the life of the soul; it converts promise to performance. Jacob wrestled with the angel of God in prayer, until his victory was confirmed. Prayer is the most potent spiritual weapon given to the children of God.

Fervent prayers will empower you to win the battles of life. When you pray like Jabez, you will receive the power to re-write your family's history. Prayer will roll-away every reproach in your business and restore your lost opportunities. The best way to build your future is by building your prayer life. In Luke 22:46, Jesus said to His disciples: ***"Why do you sleep? Rise and pray, lest you enter into temptation."*** Prayer is the greatest antidote to temptation. Through prayer, Daniel changed the course of history in his generation, and angel of God stopped the mouth of the lion. I do not know the kind of lion that is roaring against your life; the God of Daniel will appear for your sake and stop their mouths, in Jesus' name.

Prayer is the key that opens the heaven. In Luke 18:1 Jesus advised that ***"Men ought always to pray and not to faint."*** Persistent prayers will remove your name and family from evil records of darkness. It will separate you from dark cycles, witchcraft decisions and ancestral covenants. Prayers will give you the spiritual authority to crush the serpent of darkness in your foundation. The Bible says that Jesus would baptize us with the Holy Ghost and with Fire. It means that, as a Christian, your prayer life must be fire brand. The ministry of Jesus Christ was purely combatant against the works of darkness. Jesus declared that "Son of God was manifested to destroy the works of darkness" Jesus exemplified a lifestyle of prayer. He continued all night in prayers to God (Luke 6:12). He taught the apostles how to pray and the means to receive answers to prayers. Fire prayers will release power from heaven to enforce your desires. A Christian is greatest on his knees. In fact, any ministry or church that is not building your prayer life is not helping your spiritual growth. A person can wander in despair for a long time until he starts to pray the right kind of prayers. As Jesus overturned the tables of the money-changers, prayers will scatter all evil transactions working against your glory. Your voice in prayer is the greatest weapon for your turn-around breakthrough. Until you make prayer a necessity; it is difficult to fulfil destiny. Prayer will build the wall of fire around your destiny and protect you from devourers. The problems that prayers cannot solve has not been created.

Through prayer, you will put an end to all satanic oppressions. ***Psalm 7:9 "Let the wickedness of the wicked come to an end."*** The enemy would take advantage of you until you decide to be serious with prayers. Those who really desire to accomplish their glorious destiny must be prayer addicts. You must understand that there are powers that do not want you to achieve the destiny that God has purposed for you. The powers of darkness that afflicted your parents will try to hinder you, unless you decide to stop their activities through prayer warfare. The good things you wish or struggle to achieve can only be possible if you pray earnestly for divine assistance. Your emotions have no effect in the spirit realm, God works by principles and He listens to the prayers of His people. Prayer is the most valuable means to connect with God and receive help.

THE EFFICACY OF FIRE PRAYERS

Prayer reveals the deep things of God to us according to ***Daniel 2:22 "God reveals the deep and secret things, He knows what is in darkness because, light dwells with Him."*** The revelation that will turn the table to our favor is made available during prayers. There are miracles that will never happen until you pray with determination. Prayer connects you to God and unites your spirit with the Holy Ghost. It will energize your soul, open your spiritual eyes and unblock your inner ears to hear the voice of God. Prayer gives you the confidence and ability to resist the plans of your enemies. Prayer will sanitize your spiritual life and beautify your dreams. Joseph, the earthly father of Jesus Christ received divine directions through dreams, because he prayed to God. Prayer gives you the ability to function effectively in the army of the living God. Being a member of the Lord's army places you above the oppressions of all uncircumcised enemies.

Prayer mobilizes the host of heaven to intervene in our situation. When Paul and Silas prayed in the prison, an earthquake of deliverance was released from heaven to save them. Your prayers will cause confusion in the camp of your enemies. Fervent prayers will fortify you with power that will subdue your adversaries. It will release the finger of God to fight in your battlefield.

A woman came to me for prayers because of constant spiritual battles. Before we started prayers, she appealed that I should first allow her explain the problems to me. But, I told her that God knows about it better than she can imagine. So, we began to pray, after about ninety minutes of serious prayers; I told her that she can now explain what she wanted to tell me. Excitedly, she told me that everything she intended to say, that I have mentioned them in the prayer points. The Holy Spirit revealed her problems as prayer points. We gave thanks to God and she left. The next day, she called my phone with so much joy that she wanted to see me. "What happened?" I asked. She said that since the past eight months, she was able to sleep well for the first time, after my prayers. So, I encouraged her to continue with warfare prayers against the camp of her enemies, and I gave her some more powerful prayer points. **2 Samuel 22:38 says "I have pursued my enemies and destroyed them; neither did I turn back again till they were consumed."** God's power can only flow to the people who spent quality time in prayers.

Any long term problem in your life must die when you decide to pray. Prayer energizes your personal angels to perfectly execute their work of protection, and release blessings to your life. It will cut-off every negative flow in your family line and separate you from any evil inheritance. Prayer will bring out your hidden virtues and resurrect your dead potentials. It will lift up your head above terror and establish your feet on solid ground.

Prayer will bring the fourth man into your fire and empower you to rule in the midst of your enemies. It will give you access to the warehouse of the strongman, in order for you to recover your stolen possessions. Prayers will make you operate in the realm that is higher than your enemies. It will reveal the secret of your enemies to you; and your victory will manifest. Prayer is not an option for Christians, it is a necessity! Persistent prayers will make heaven to respect your voice and obey your commands. Heaven released fire to respect the voice of Elijah. At the voice of Moses, the ground opened and swallowed up his enemies. Joshua commanded the sun and moon to stand still; they obeyed and stood till until he defeated his enemies. ***Matthew 18:18 Whatever you bind on earth would be bound in heaven, and whatever you loose on earth will be loosed in heaven.*** I pray that your voice will not be a stranger to Heaven in Jesus name.

You must understand that certain people are not comfortable with your promotions and your celebrations are great offences to them. Most times, your worst enemies are the same people that you have helped. At times, the people you worked so hard to ensure their success are the ones struggling to pull you down, even though you have not offended them. Your kindness to people can become an offence to them. You need to engage in prayer warfare so that all evil plans fashioned against you, will end in painful failure. Powers reporting you to strongman of darkness and those digging evil pits to bury your glory, shall be destroyed by fire when you engage in violent prayers. God establishes the word of His servants who pray to

Him day and night (Psalm 55:17). Your spiritual antennas must be higher than that of your enemies. Christianity is spiritual enrolment in the army of the Living God. Your identity as a soldier of Jesus Christ is your son ship authority over the powers of darkness. Prayers will clothe you with the mercy of God and the enemy will never consume you. Jeremiah 51:20 confirms that through prayers, you become the spiritual tool in God's hand for His miracles in your family and community.

Apostle Paul says that ***"his desire is that Christians should pray everywhere lifting holy hands to God (1 Timothy 2:8)".*** I used this principle in year 1999, and it opened my door of blessings to the glory of God. Fulfilment of great destinies are exclusively for those who devote quality time to prayers. Take note that great ideas will always come to your mind during prayers. When you decide to engage in prayer warfare, everything in your life will be gloriously transformed.

KEEP YOUR PRAYER FIRE BURNING

If you allow the enemy to destroy your prayer life, your Christian life is dead. A man who refuses to pray is actually refusing to grow. Prayer is the only nutrient for spiritual growth. A prayer-less Christian is like a warrior without weapons just as a sword inside its sheath is meaningless in the battlefield. Those who prayed in the Bible did not fail in any battle. Daniel prayed and received the excellent Spirit of God. Jesus prayed to increase the faith of Peter (Luke 22:31-32) so he could destroy the desire of Satan concerning his life. The earthquake of deliverance intervened to rescue Paul and Silas from prison, because they prayed. When Esther prayed, she received favour from the king and delivered her people from impending danger. Prayer destroys fears and oppressions. Jehoshaphat prayed, and angel of God fought his battle and destroyed his strong enemy. Prayer has always delivered me from conspiracy and from envious enemies. If you can pray always, you will certainly prevail against all battles and fears of life. Prayer to God, is assuredly the master key to victory, breakthroughs and divine settlement.

Prayer will command blessings to your storehouse and fill your mouth with testimonies. Agility in prayer will qualify you as an instrument in God's hand for His work in your generation. Prayer can heal terminal sicknesses, and solve problems that money cannot solve. Through prayer, you can receive wisdom. ***Deuteronomy 34:9 "Joshua received spirit of wisdom because Moses laid hand upon his head.*** " Prayer will fortify the spiritual pillars that will uphold the glory of your destiny. It will overhaul your spiritual life and magnetize the mercy of God into your affairs.

Spiritual violence through prayer is the only language that the enemy understands. Until you decide to pray harder, the enemies of your soul will not respect you. When Hannah prayed, God opened her womb and gave her a son as she desired. Prayer has opened the eyes of the blind, unblocked the deaf ears and loosed the tongue of the dumb. Peter prayed for the cripple at the beautiful gate and the lame man began to walk. Prayer will raise a rich man from the dust and a beggar out of the dunghill. It possesses the power that changes every situation.

Prayer gives you extra-ordinary privileges and uncommon opportunities. It makes the unknown to become the anointed. Prayer brings peace into troubled marriages and rekindle love between couples. Those who are lamenting about their marriages should pray down the fire of God to consume all strangers in the garden of their marital destiny. Prayer is the master key to financial turnaround and marital bliss. Prayer will evacuate all demonic influence and destroy all ancestral covenants. Prayer will connect you to your ordained helpers. It will make ways in your wilderness and rivers in your desert. Prayer equip you with power and confidence to excel in life.

PRAYING FOR GOD'S INTERVENTION

Note that God does not force His way into peoples' situations except you invite Him through prayers. **Revelation 3:20 "Behold, I stand at the door and knock. If anyone hears My voice and opens the door, I will come in to him and dine with him, and he with Me."** God has given the earth to the sons of men. Until you speak to your challenges, nothing will happen. When you decide to stand, then God will stand with you. Until the children of Israel cried to God in prayers, the taskmasters of Egypt subjected them to sorrows and hard bondage. Prayer will send deliverer to your situation and reveal heavenly strategies that will ensure your liberty.

The problems of life are the knees that must bow at the mention of the name, JESUS. Prayers will give you the mind of a winner and imaginations of a warrior. It will deflate the confidence of the proud boasting against you. Prayer will transport you to the realm that favour will meet you from all sides. Because you pray, where other people fail, you will achieve resounding success. Your blessings need your prayers to be permanent. Your fruitfulness and marital glory need your prayers. Your spouse needs your prayers, whether you have met him/her or not.

Prayer will open your eyes to see possibilities in every difficulty. It will give you the confidence that the enemy will not write the last chapter of your life. Your foundation needs prayer to purge it of all ancestral pollution. I pray that God will release special anointing into your life and every yoke of satanic delay, afflictions and demotions, shall be broken by fire in Jesus name.

Your business need your prayers to expand and to flourish. You need prayers for God to preserve your life and establish your goings. Your dream life need your prayers to protect it from spiritual night raiders, dream polluters and Luciferian planters. Your prayers will build the hedge of fire around your possessions against the activities of the roaring lion (1 Peter 5:8).

WAYS TO BOOST YOUR PRAYER ENERGY

1. Ensure that your life is devoid of sin.
2. Always meditate on the word of God.
3. Be a prayer addict and fast regularly.
4. Have a close relationship with the Holy Spirit; try to praise and worship God always.
5. Read books that teach on prayer, and make out time to pray regularly on daily basis.

6. Learn warfare songs, Holy Ghost fire songs, scriptural faith declarations and warfare prayer points.
7. Trust in God with all your heart, have faith in His mercies and possibilities.

Great power is released when you pray with the word of God. Where the word of a king is, there is power. Men of prayers are the same as men of Faith; they are always great. You cannot practice great faith without exercising the word of God through prayers. ***1 Corinthians 9:26 "Therefore I run thus: not with uncertainty. Thus I fight: not as one who beats the air."*** Jesus says that "he that is born of the spirit is spirit." It means that the Spirit of God in our lives as Christians has equipped us for spiritual warfare, against all satanic spirits. When Jesus commissioned the Apostles in ***Matthew 10:1-2 'He gave them power over unclean spirits'.***

We are God's special emissaries on earth and we are seated with Christ above all principalities and powers.

THINGS THAT LIMIT YOUR PRAYER LIFE

(i) FEAR: "God has not given us the spirit of fear, but of power and of love and of a sound mind." (2 Timothy 1:7). Fear is the opposite of faith and the quencher of spiritual fire.

(ii) POVERTY OF GOD'S WORD: The word of God is the spiritual nutrient that grows your prayer life. Your faith increases as you meditate and read the Bible always. Joshua 1:8 advises on the necessity of reading and meditating on the word of God.

(iii) ANGER: A person who gets angry easily cannot grow spiritually. Anyone who is hot-tempered is naturally proud because; anger is an offshoot of pride.

(iv) DISCOURAGEMENT: This is the worst form of laziness. David encouraged himself in the Lord (1 Samuel 30:6). You must learn to encourage yourself if you really want to fulfill your divine destiny. Discouragement is the enemy of persistence. The Bible says that ***"the effectual fervent prayer of the righteous avails much."*** You need consistency and determination in your prayer in order to obtain your desired testimonies.

(v) HAVE A FORGIVING HEART: **Matthew 6:12** ***"And forgive us our debts, as we forgive our debtors."*** It is written that 'If I regard iniquity in my heart, the lord will not hear me. The state of your heart will determine how far your prayers will go. Jesus says ***"If you do not forgive men their trespasses, God will not forgive you."*** Forgiveness will liberate your heart and attract God's mercy into your situation.

Prayer is the last hope of every living soul. God of the suddenly is alive and actively ready to deliver you from all troubles. When situations seem hopeless, put on the armour of prayer, it is the last hope of every living soul. Call upon God on the day of trouble, He will deliver you; and you will glorify Him. The Almighty God is our last resort; His intervention changes every situation. Pray your life and your possessions out of evil spiritual control. Your voice of prayer has the power to swallow any voice accusing your breakthroughs. We wrestle in prayer against principalities, powers and rulers of darkness of this world. ***Ephesians 6:12-16 "For we wrestle not against flesh and blood, but against principalities, against powers, against the rulers of the darkness of this world, against spiritual wickedness in high places."*** Only Jesus is the answer, until you come to God and cast your burdens unto Him, all struggles are mere waste of time.

Isaiah 10:27 "It shall come to pass in that day, that his burden will be taken away from your shoulder, and his yoke from your neck, and the yoke will be destroyed because of the anointing oil." If you have been to a poultry farm, you will see how chickens are kept in cages, with boundaries that they can never cross. In the same way, some foundational and witchcraft powers have built spiritual cages to limit and control people's lives. They control your mind and make some habits difficult for you to break. They join you to wrong and destructive friends and prevent you from receiving favour at the right places. Prayer is more powerful than atomic energy. It will transform your soul and reshape your life. Prayer is spiritual sanitation; it develops your inner-man to receive from the Holy Ghost. If you can pray without ceasing, no circumstance will defeat you. Show me a man who pray always and I will tell you that his life is too hot for the enemy to handle. I pray that God in His infinite mercy will revive your prayer life and make you a spiritual champion in the name of Jesus Christ. AMEN.

PRAYER POINTS

1. Any envious witchcraft attacking my prosperity, summersault and die, in Jesus' name
2. Where is the Lord God of Elijah? Arise, change my story to glory in the name of Jesus.
3. Evil powers in my foundation deciding the affairs of my life, die by fire, in Jesus' name.
4. Powers waging war against my breakthroughs, catch fire and die, in Jesus' name.
5. Satanic ceremony performed to cage my destiny, be destroyed by fire, in Jesus' name.
6. Powers assigned to execute evil judgment against me, fall down and die, in Jesus' name.
7. Any power, any spirit, equipped by the devil to cut short my life, catch fire and die, in Jesus' name.
8. Any wicked finger, pointing against my life, wither by fire in the name of Jesus Christ.
9. Any power, any spirit, challenging the goodness of God in my life, fall down and die in the name of Jesus.
10. Any padlock of darkness locking up my finances, break by fire in Jesus name.
11. Evil meetings held to disgrace me, be scattered unto desolation in Jesus' name.
12. Evil chain that has tied down any area of my life, be broken by fire, in Jesus' name.
13. Every satanic conspiracy against my destiny, scatter by fire, in Jesus' name.
14. Evil brooms sweeping away my goodness, catch fire, burn to ashes in Jesus' name.

CHAPTER SEVEN

The Great Commandment

The King of the whole earth desires that we live rightly for the fulfillment of our destinies. Therefore, He provides a set of rules and appropriate doctrines to regulate our actions as His children. These commandments are the rules of conduct for effective relationship with God. ***Proverbs 6:23 "For the commandment is a lamp, and the law a light; reproofs of instruction are the way of life."*** To Israel, the law revealed the nature and principles of God. When God issued the law he declared from the creator's infinite wisdom, what He valued as just, righteous and equitable. God gave the ten commandments to Moses when he called him to lead the Children of Israel. Obedience to these commandments was necessary for God to be with them.

Therefore, the law was our guardian to bring us to Christ that we might be justified by faith.

Our Lord Jesus summarized the commandments and identified the most important requirement.

Matthew 22:35-40 ***"Then one of them, a lawyer, asked Jesus a question, testing Him, and saying, "Teacher, which is the great commandment in the law?" Jesus said to him, 'You shall love the Lord your God with all your heart, with all your soul, and with all your mind.'***

This is the first and great commandment. And the second is like it: 'You shall love your neighbor as yourself.' On these two commandments hang all the Law and the Prophets."

Jesus emphasized that the great and foremost commandment is that ***"you shall love the Lord your God with all your heart, with all your soul, and with all your mind".*** Love for God is the prime focus and heart-beat of all the commandments. ***Jesus says, "If you love me, keep my commandments" (John 14:15).*** That is, if we truly love God, we will keep His commandments. Love for God gives us the right motives to obey and attend to the desires of God as expressed in the scriptures. God reveals Himself to those who love him, and attend to their requests. Jesus instructed that we must Love God with all our hearts because the control center of our words and actions is the heart. ***Luke 6:45 "A good man out of the good treasure of his heart brings forth good; and an evil man out of the evil treasure of his heart brings forth evil. For out of the abundance of the heart his mouth speaks"***

Everything in the old testament is about laws, doctrines, commandments and visions of the prophets. All these depend on the great and foremost commandment of love. Love is supreme!

Love is the spiritual principles that will make you serve God without stress. Bible says "I will deliver you from your struggles" This privilege of divine settlement is exclusively for those who love God with all their hearts. God will fight your battles; He will hiss against your enemies and break yokes of limitations in your life because you obey the commandment of love. Peace reigns in the atmosphere of love. Anywhere you find true love, it produces unity, joy and progress.

God wants us to love Him with all our soul, with the deepest level of intimacy, holding nothing back. The person or object whom you love with all your heart will define your true personality. Total love for God gives you His divine nature. Loving God with all your heart means that your first spiritual loyalty is to Him. When you acknowledge God in all your ways; He will direct your steps and regulate your actions, thoughts and decisions. He who hears the commandments of God and keeps them and doeth them is the person that loves God.-John 14:21

The teachings of Jesus Christ give us the power and motivation to love, trust and obey God.

Jesus gave a commandment that encompassed all other commandments of God in two simple sentences: "Love God" and "Love your Neighbor."

To effectively practice the love of God, you must look for positive ways to enhance the life and prosperity of your neighbors. Loving God empowers us to love our brothers and sisters.

Without love for God, the external observance of other commandments becomes an empty form.

LOVE YOUR NEIGHBOUR

1 John 4:19-21 "If someone says, "I love God," and hates his brother, he is a liar; for he who does not love his brother whom he has seen, how can he love God whom he has not seen? And this commandment we have from Him: that he who loves God must love his brother also." One major proof of loving God is that we must show sincere and sacrificial love to our brothers and sisters. Until you love God as you should, you will never love your neighbor as you could. If you truly love your neighbor, you will not murder him, you will not steal from him and you will not gossip against him. Love for others keeps us in the light of God and releases divine promises into our lives. Jesus explained the exact scriptural meaning of love your neighbor in **Matthew 7:12** ***"Therefore, whatever you want men to do to you, do also to them, for this is the Law and the Prophets."*** The act of treating others as you want to be treated is the correct definition of **the law and the prophets**. This is also referred to as the "Golden Rule."

Loving your neighbor means that you will do to him whatever you would do for yourself.

We are created to Love God and extend the character of love to one another. Bible says that you must not hate your brother in your heart. Hatred will blindfold you spiritually; it will position a person in spiritual darkness. Hatred and resentment will close a person's heaven. His prayers will be mocked by the enemy. Doing evil to your brothers and sisters will energize the enemies against you. It will make a person fail where he is supposed to succeed. Whoever hates his brother is a murderer. The bible says that haters grope around in darkness; it means that they stay perpetually in confusion. Hatred is more dangerous than witchcraft. When God anointed Jesus of Nazareth, with Holy Ghost and with power, He went about doing good, healing all that were oppressed because God was with Him. The Spirit of God in you will make you to do good to others. If you keep the principles of love, your life will matter so much to God, you will become the apple of God's eyes. So many problems will be solved even before you pray about it. The greatest freedom for your soul is love; the greatest personal security and wisdom of life, is love. We have to show love to God and prove it by love to man, so that we can fulfill our destinies.

So many people are limited and their circumstances are not in conformity with divine destiny for their lives. Their limitations and stagnancy are not caused by any evil power. It is the character of wickedness, vengefulness and hatred that they have allowed to bear evil fruits in their lives.

The principle of staying in the love of God is by loving another person. To prove that you truly love God is to manifest that love for your brothers and sisters. The practice of Love makes light to shine in your darkness. When the light of God goes forth for your sake, woe betides the enemy that wants to stand against your progress. The positive impact of your love on others will move God to satisfy your desires with good things; and crown you with compassion.

GOD IS LOVE: Means that the character and nature of God is love. As children of God, created in His own image and likeness, we have the innate capacity to show love. The sacrifice of Jesus is the evidence of God's love to humanity. We are commanded to replicate God's love to our neighbors; this is key to enjoy the mercies of God, healing and abundant kindness from above.

God is completeness of light, and he who loves, stays in the light. Love is key to glorious living!

Jesus advised ***in John 13:34-34 "I give you a new commandment, love one another, you must love one another, just as I have loved you, if you love one another, everyone will know that you are my disciples."*** Love is our first identity card as disciples of Jesus Christ. It is the only key that opens the door of answered prayers. Obeying the commandment of God means that we completely trust Jesus as our good shepherd. Christ in us is our hope of glory; without Him, we can do nothing. Your ability, intelligence, capacity and dexterity of your hands can achieve nothing without Jesus Christ. It is written that "Man at his best state, is all together vanity."

The flesh profits nothing; it is the spirit that quickens. Love is the only key to receive help and mercies of God. It quickens the attainment of our promotions and actualization of our blessings.

1 John 3:17 "But whoever has this world's goods, and sees his brother in need, and shuts up his heart from him, how does the love of

God abide in him?" The proof of our love for God is how we sacrificially practice same to the humanity around us.

THE HUNTER'S PROOF OF LOVE

A man has a friend, and the same man has only one brother. The man was a very great, talented and prosperous hunter. Unfortunately, his friend poisoned his mind against his only brother.

He told the hunter that his brother hates him so much; and he believed his friend to the extent that he stopped talking to his brother. The two brothers became enemies; they were not talking to each other and they avoid every opportunity of meeting face to face.

The hunter goes to the forest every night and come back with plenty of bushmeat. His best friend would bring other friends and they enjoyed the meat together. They continued telling the hunter that his brother is a wizard, a wicked and occultist man that do not want his progress.

One day, the hunter advised himself, he said, **"I have only one brother, but year after year my friends enjoy the fruits of my labour and my only brother is forsaken."** So, he planned this strategy: He went to the bush for hunting, killed a very big animal and covered it with leaves. At about 3:00am in the night, he rushed back to the village and knocked at the door of his friend. His best friend was surprised by the unusual knock at that hour of the night, "hope all is well" the friend asked. "No, all is not well, I have just killed a human being in the bush" replied the hunter. He pleaded with his friend to accompany him to the bush and thinker with him how they could solve the problem together. The same friend, who had pretended to love him so much, asked him "have you told your brother?" The hunter reminded him that he had not been in talking terms with his brother for many years. But his best friend insisted, "Go to your brother, I want to sleep with my children." He locked the door against the hunter.

The hunter was shockingly disappointed! He moved to his brother's house and knocked at the door, shouting "open the door, open the door." The brother heard his voice and opened the door "what is the problem?" he asked. "I have just killed a human being in the bush" replied the hunter. "I thought it was an animal" the hunter continued to explain. But the brother quickly interrupted, he asked "Hope you have not told this to anybody?" The hunter said "NO."

The brother quickly followed him to the bush, consoling and comforting him that they will solve the problem together. An adage says "On the day of true brothers, agony and woes are nullified."

When they moved close to the location in the bush, the hunter pointed at the animal covered with leaves, "that is the human being, I mistakenly killed him and covered him with leaves" the hunter wept bitterly. But his brother opened the leaves and shouted, "this is animal, not a human being."

The hunter came forward and hugged his brother. He said "now, I know that you truly love me" They reconciled and rebuilt great love for each other. Bible says "How pleasant it will be for brothers to live together in harmony. God values that we forgive and live peaceably with our brothers. ***Matthew 5:23-24 "Therefore if you bring your gift to God at the altar, and there remember that your brother has something against you, leave your gift there before the altar, and go your way. First be reconciled to your brother, and then come and offer your gift."***

The standard of the scripture is that for God to accept your gift, you must reconcile and live happily with your brothers and sisters. Love is the essence of the spirit of the gospel.

Brotherly love translates you from spiritual death to the abundant live of Christ, with benefits of inheritance of the saints. If a person says that he is in the light but hates his brother, such person is in darkness even until now. Heaven of breakthroughs will always open to those who genuinely show love to others. Some people have ignorantly multiplied their problems and blocked the heavens of their blessings due to wicked devices against their neighbors.

In the Lord's Prayer, Jesus says **"forgive me my trespasses, as I forgive those who trespass against me."** Love is the only key that opens spiritual doors in churches, families and nations.

If you fail to love your neighbors, you are denying yourself the love and kindness of God.

Love will qualify you to enjoy the fellowship of heavenly angels and gift of the Holy Spirit.

The power of God will cause resurrection into every dead area of your life. Love tends to life, it brings peace and restoration. If you desire fulfilment of great destiny, obey and practice love.

1 John 3:14 ***"We know that we have passed from death to life, because we love the brethren. He who does not love his brother abides in death."*** Those who hate their brothers suffer spiritual death in prayers, businesses, marriages, talents, profession and several vital areas of life. Anyone who disobeys the commandment of love breaks the hedge of God's coverage, so they face multiple attacks from the kingdom of darkness. To enjoy the presence and protection of God, you must love your neighbor. If other things fail, love will never fail because God is love. What you do to others determine what happens in your life. Bible says "to the merciful God will show Himself merciful." It means that, to receive the mercies of God, you must be merciful to others. The best thing that will cement and consolidate our relationship with God is to love our neighbor as ourselves. Perfect love casts out fear. We must allow love to rule in our gatherings in Church and in our families. It will position us to inherit blessings and glory from God as children of Abraham. Bible says that children of Abraham will always receive help from God.

PURE RELIGION

James 1:27 "Pure and undefiled religion before God and the Father is this: to visit orphans and widows in their trouble, and to keep oneself unspotted from the world."

There are religions that are spiritually tainted with iniquity. Some religions are defiled and there are religions that are not pure. But pure religion declares that you must share with the poor and the needy. There is healing, freedom, prosperity, light and grace in the practice of love.

One day, in a revelation, God showed me a young woman. She was praying so fervently and passionately for a particular thing. She was so determined in prayers and her blessing were just in front of her, but she could not collect them. God showed me that her blessings had been released long ago but her hands were tightfisted. In the revelation, I saw helpless people before her and the Lord said "If she can open her hands to give to these people, all these blessings shall come to her, and she will stop the endless sweating and struggling in prayers."

In fact, the answers to our prayers are easily accessed when we open our hands to help our neighbors in the best way we can. ***Proverbs 3:27-28 "Do not withhold good from those to whom it is due, when it is in the power of your hand to do so. Do not say to your neighbor, "Go, and come back, and tomorrow I will give it," when you have it with you."*** We must endeavor to help our brothers and friends in times of need. You will receive faster help from God when you help others, by giving sacrificially to meet their needs. God is the greatest rewarder of all kindness shown to humanity. Jesus has called us to love our neighbor with an extravagant, generous love, acceptance and forgiveness. When we do this, people will recognize that we are children of our Father in Heaven. Love originates from God and anyone who loves is born of God and knows God. But anyone who does not love does not know God, for God is love.

The key to honour and lifting up is in love. You will receive divine interventions, blessings and helps from unexpected quarters when you give freely to others. Love is the greatest bulldozer that demolishes every obstacle. Love will open doors of breakthroughs and release the deliverance of God into our lives. Blessed is he who considers the poor; the Lord will deliver him in time of trouble. Love does no harm to a neighbor; therefore, love is fulfillment of the law.

We need to intentionally place high value on people, seeing them as persons created in the image and likeness of God. See your friends, spouses, colleagues, and relatives as object to be loved; not an obstacle to overcome. You must truly love all the people that God brings into your life.

So many people believe in revenge and retaliation, but Jesus teaches the principle of forgiveness, instead of revenge. You can truly become extravagant in love by going above and beyond in your generosity. ***Matthew 5:43-44 "You have heard that it was said, 'You shall love your neighbor and hate your enemy.' But I say to you, love your enemies, bless those who curse you, do good to those who hate you, and pray for those who spitefully use you and persecute you"*** We live in a world where few people know how to connect in deep and meaningful relationships with one another. To make our environments habitable and happier for all; we need to rediscover the art of neighboring. Love is the foundation for unity and peace in environments.

The essence of commandments is mainly to love and obey God as the only true Lord; and to respect one another with earnest commitment to the prosperity and care for others.

Galatian 5:14 "For all the law is fulfilled in one word, even in this: "You shall love your neighbor as yourself." Give to him who asks you, and from him who wants to borrow from you do not turn away. Love for one another is the proof of discipleship. It takes a humble heart to love his neghbour. Jesus washed the feet of His disciples to show how a leader should love his followers, and he advised that we do same to others. This is a scriptural guideline for us to effectively practice love for one another. ***Leviticus 19:15-16 "You shall do no injustice in judgment. You shall not be partial to the poor, nor honor the person of the mighty. In righteousness you shall judge your neighbor. 16 You shall not go about as a talebearer among your people; nor shall you take a stand against the life of your neighbor: I am the Lord."***

The habitation of God is full of justice and we are commanded to uphold fairness in decision; avoid gossips and do not bear false witness against your neighbor. Disobedience to these vital commandments attracts the wrath of God against people. If we humbly serve God in obedience to these commandments, we shall spend our days in prosperity and our lives in pleasures.

THE ROYAL LAW – Laws of the Kingdom.

For Christians to live with authority as priests and kings, enjoying the spiritual powers and gifts of God; we must keep the royal law. This is the spiritual statute that establishes the promises of God in our lives. Once you fulfill the royal law, you enjoy the inheritances of Christ as of right.

James 2:8 If you really fulfill the royal law according to the Scripture, "You shall love your neighbor as yourself," You do well. This releases the grace to partake in the heritage of the servants of the Lord, whose righteousness is of the Lord. The royal states ***thus "You***

shall love your neighbout as yourself." Some blessings are delayed, hindered or denied when people fail to keep the royal law. If you obey the commandment of love, God will release His grace into the affairs of your life and make you a spectacle to many. Loving God is an internal passion of the soul; but it comes to expression when you love others. Therefore, loving others is the outward manifestation, visible expression, practical demonstration and fulfillment of the Laws of God. You must keep the royal law in order to experience the raw power of God that delivers from struggles, fears and troubles.

True love puts you at the center of God's power; It qualifies you for divine partnership with the host of heaven. God's angels will bear you up in their hands and you will not dash your feet against any stone of failure or regrets. Your generous actions to the creation of God is the only evidence that you truly love God. One day, Jesus asked Peter, "do you love me more than these?" Peter answered "I love you Lord" Jesus instructed him thus "Feed my lamb." Love is not in word but in practice. When Peter declared his love for the Lord, Jesus instructed him "feed my sheep." You must endeavor to give your best help to benefit others. When you truly maintain a charitable and peaceful relationship with others, it will keep your feet in the light of God's kingdom. ***1 John 3:17 "But if anyone has enough money to live well and sees a brother or sister in need and refuses to help–how can God's love be in that person?"***

A very sick man went to his rich brother, pleading for financial assistance to treat his ailment. But his brother kept complaining that he does not have enough money; insisting that releasing such money will affect his business. The man died prematurely due to scarcity of funds required to buy drugs. How can his belligerent brother, who could not sacrifice his comfort to save a brother, confidently say that he loves God. True love is validated and consolidated by sacrifice.

You must be committed to sacrifice your convenience, eschew pride and give part of your possession for the benefit of another person. Jesus advised that the whatever assistance you render to the least of the people, is given to God. This proves that generosity is service to God and also to humanity. Charity attracts mercies from God and delivers people from works of darkness. Givers never lack and the hands of a giver is always on top. You are created to contribute something tangible for the betterment of humanity during your period of existence in the land of the living. Your kindness can safe souls from death, it can reshape destiny and give hope to the hopeless. The ministry of Jesus Christ was founded on love for the people. He went about doing good, healing the oppressed, and setting at liberty all those who were bruised by the devil. The blessings given to you by God is supposed to benefit the needy and support some people towards fulfilment of destinies. Love is patient and kind; it thinks no evil and endures all things.

The world will unite in happiness, if people adapts the habit of helping one another in sincerity.

The whole Law and the Prophets and all our Father's plans and acts hang on these two great sovereign purposes of God; that we love God totally and love our neighbors unconditionally.

THINGS THAT YOUR GIFTS WILL DO FOR YOU

How do you want to spend the remaining days of your life? What changes do you pray for, in order to live better days ahead of you? He who gives to the poor is lending to God.

If you are willing and obedient to commandment of love, you will eat the good of the land.

Here are four (4) great benefits that you receive when you treat people with heart of generosity:

1. <u>Your gift will build an altar for you and raise spiritual voice of mercy.</u> The voice of the Lord is powerful; The voice of the Lord divides the flames of fire. The voice of the Lord is full of majesty. Your gifts will shield you with spiritual defense against accusers and wasters. ***Psalm 27:2 "When the wicked came against me to eat up my flesh, my enemies and foes, they stumbled and fell."*** God gives prosperity to all those who help the needy and rescues them from their enemies. He specially defends them from strife of tongues and from evil judgements.

If someone is in hopeless situation and was about to give-up when you extend kindness that restores hope and solution; the person prays to God from deepest of his heart, to bless you. God attends to such prayers speedily. Those who earnestly provides help to others in need, either by services or gifts, for the sake of God, are always favoured with bountiful blessings and health. One good thing is that their children are always delivered from the plans of the wicked. ***Psalms 41:2 "The Lord will preserve him and keep him alive, and he will be blessed on the earth; God will not deliver him to the will of his enemies."***

2. Your gift will open the heaven of blessings and release God's word into your situation.

   As God remembered his covenant with Abraham and helped the children of Israel, your good works towards others will attract the watchful eyes of God, to preserve your children from destructions and oppressions. Your Charity will protect your gifts from the rod of the wicked.

   The Spirit of the Lord will lift a standard against any flood of the enemy confronting your life.

   It will defend you from conspiracy and save your possessions from wasting powers of the devil.

   1 Timothy 6:17-18 "Command those who are rich in this present age not to be haughty, nor to trust in uncertain riches but in the living God, who gives us richly all things to enjoy. Let them do good, that they be rich in good works, ready to give, willing to share" God loves a cheerful giver. Besides, God is able to make every blessing of yours overflow for you, so that in every situation you will always have all you need for any good work.

3. If you give liberally, your gift will untie your hands and empower it for more breakthroughs. The act of giving will deliver your hands from bewitchment and close evil holes in your palms. ***Proverbs 11:24-25 "There is one who scatters, yet increases more; and there is one who withholds more than is right, but it leads to poverty. The generous soul will be made rich, and he who waters will also be watered himself."*** We are instructed

to imitate Christ both in actions and conversations. Was Christ thinking only about Himself when He died on the cross? No!

The scripture makes it clear that when your heart is set on blessing others, God will bless you in the process. The more you give, the more comes back to you, because God is the greatest giver in the universe. ***Luke 3:10-11 So the people asked him, saying, "What shall we do then?" He answered and said to them, "He who has two tunics, let him give to him who has none; and he who has food, let him do likewise."*** You must try to be someone's sunshine when their skies are grey. We make a living by what we get but, we make a life by what we give.

4. ***Your gifts on earth will send deposits to your spiritual account in heaven.*** When you open your heart to giving, angels fly to your door. Your hands will be anointed with the power of God; for healing, blessing and deliverance. When you give cheerfully to improve the lives of others, you represent God in their situation. It means that you position your life and possessions in the Light of God. Your generous gifts to the needy will protect your life and properties from the devourer. Troubles that injuriously affects others in your line of business will not touch yours. Hazardous occurrences will not destroy your properties and you will have peace roundabout.

   Surprisingly, you will receive idea or revelation that will solve your worries and terminate all confusions. You will become a friend of God and your spiritual gifts will be active and fruitful.

1 John 2:10-11 "Those who love their brothers and sisters are living in the light. There is nothing in them to make them fall into sin. Those who hate a brother or sister are in the darkness. They walk around in the darkness. They don't know where they are going. The darkness has made them blind". God is love, and the person who stays in love stays in God, and God stays in him. Jesus warned, "Be on your guard against all kinds of greed; a man's life does not consist in the abundance of his possessions." God's purpose for entrusting you with more riches and possessions is that you should give even more to the needy and also to His work.

It is type of praises to God, if you appreciate His creation by assisting to make others live better.

God will make you rich in every way so that you can be generous on every occasion, and your generosity will result in thanksgiving to God. Apparently, the same God who supplies seed to the sower and bread for food will also supply and increase your store of seed and will enlarge the harvest of your righteousness. Note that when Zacchaeus became a believer, he gave 50 percent of his assets to the poor, in demonstration of his thankfulness for salvation in Christ (Luke 19:8).

HOW YOU CAN SHOW LOVE TO YOUR NEIGHBOUR

Better a dish of vegetables with love than a fattened calf with hatred. Love is key to harmony.

1. PURE HEART; FREE MIND*:* "You shall not hate your brother in your heart. You shall not take vengeance, nor bear any grudge against the children of your people, but you shall love your neighbor as yourself" Leviticus 19:16-18. The world will certainly be more secured and peaceful for all, if we imbibe the commandment of love and forgiveness for one another. Forgiveness is one great attribute that must be practiced by anyone who desires to enjoy the Love of God. It is the gateway to access the presence of God. If you forgive offences of others, God will forgive yours and attend to your prayers graciously. Bible says that if I regard iniquity in my heart, the Lord will not hear me. It proves that bearing grudges or hatred to our neighbors will negatively affect our fellowship with God and hinder answers to prayers. ***Matthew 18:15 "If thy brother shall trespass against thee, go and tell him his fault between thee and him alone: if he shall hear thee, thou hast gained thy brother."*** Forgiveness is sign of humility and wisdom of God.
2. CHARITY means the voluntary giving of help to those in need. ***Isaiah 58:7 "I prefer that you share your food with the hungry and to provide the poor wanderer with shelter— when you see the naked, clothe them, and do not turn away from your own***

flesh and blood?" The best way for you to attract divine help into your life is by helping others. The Samaritan was on his way to somewhere, but he stopped when he saw the man in need. We live in a fast-paced world where it is easy to overlook the needs of others. But we need to be proactive and extend the duty of care to those who are around us. The Apostles ensured that the Church practiced generosity towards the needy; people sold their possessions and brought the proceeds at the apostles' feet; and they distributed to each as anyone had need.

Our Lord Jesus Christ was observant to notice the need of others and He help them speedily.

Matthew 9:36 "But when He saw the multitudes, He was moved with compassion for them, because they were weary and scattered, like sheep having no shepherd." We must do likewise to help those in need around us. Kindness is a seed for better tomorrow, it never dies. The person you help today can be your savior tomorrow. Your sacrificial help can save someone from the gate of grave and deliver his soul from grip of frustration. Those who desire regular fellowship with the Spirit of God must effectively show love to neighbors including brothers and sisters.

3. <u>FORGIVE ONE ANOTHER:</u> Love and forgiveness liberates the mind and cements your relationship with God. ***Colossians 3:13 "bearing with one another, and forgiving one another, if anyone has a complaint against another; even as Christ forgave you, so you also must do."*** It is natural to encounter offences from people around us. In fact, your best effort to please someone can become offensive to the person, without your knowledge. In same way, people can mistakenly offend you and may not even know that they have wronged you. The discretion of a man makes him slow to anger, and his glory is to overlook a transgression. Long and enduring relationships are usually made of those who forgives, and overlook offences. They do not condemn people for their mistakes, instead they proffer corrections and solutions for progress.

   To enjoy peaceful and lovely relationships, we must maintain the habit of forgiveness.

1 Peter 3:8-9 "Finally, all of you be of one mind, having compassion for one another; love as brothers, be tenderhearted, be courteous; not returning evil for evil or reviling for reviling, but on the contrary blessing, knowing that you were called to this, that you may inherit a blessing." It means that God has graciously designed great blessings for us, if we forgive and show unconditional love to our neighbors. Being vindictive over offences will cause regrets, tragedy and destruction of destiny.

4. UNITY: The Church should have the attitude of working together, apostles were united in Love. **Acts 2:44-46** ***"All the believers were together; and everything they had was for the use of all. They sold their things and divided the money among the believers. They gave each person what he needed. And they, continuing daily with one accord in the temple, and breaking bread from house to house, did eat their meat with gladness and singleness of heart."*** The Apostles were all with one accord in one place, with one mind and one purpose; when suddenly there came a sound from heaven as of a rushing mighty wind, and it filled all the house where they were sitting. The Spirit of God will always manifest awesome powers in our congregations when the Church is united in love. I am hoping and praying that Churches will be united as One Big Family, sharing and rejoicing together and helping one another in all things. ***Galatians 6:10 "As we have therefore opportunity, let us do good unto all men, especially unto them who are of the household of faith"*** Nowadays, some church leaders have become obsessed with material things and indulging more on worldly pleasures; undermining the essence of love. We should learn to give generously to God's work and also to fellow Christians without a grudging heart. It is more blessed to give than receive.

The larger our hearts and the wider our hands, the larger the picture we paint of God's character. When we give sacrificially, above and beyond what is comfortable and easy, we are expressing our faith and trust in God to provide for us and our families. Many Christians have discovered the joy of casting their crumbs of bread upon the waters and multiple loaves returning after many days (Ecclesiastes 11:1). It's such a joy to see God fulfill His promise of provision when we obey Him. David sang: "What shall I render to the Lord for all his benefits towards me?" (Psalms 116:12). Giving in a right spirit is act of worship. It is rendering Him a tribute of praise. It is saying. "You gave me everything and here is a small expression of my gratitude and praise for all your good gifts." Then, the Lord your God will bless you in all your work and in everything you do. Jesus says that whatever you give to the least of brethren, you are giving unto God. We must learn that it is not only Pastors that represent God, He is creator of all human beings. He enjoins us to give to the poor, help the sick, shelter the homeless and give comfort to the distressed. Some people will see their brother dying of hunger and refuse to help; but they will pack much money to the Pastor begging him to pray for them to get more blessings.

The continent of Africa will be much better if church leaders will consider helping the poor as priority. The insensitivity of political leaders will have less devastating effect on the lives of Christians, if the vital amenities like education and healthcare are made easier by the Churches.

These practices of love will make sinners to accept Jesus Christ and embrace the gospel faster.

THE PRAYER POINTS:

1. I receive the light of God to honour Him with all my heart in Jesus name.
2. Dark consultations fashioned to rubbish my destiny, scatter by fire in Jesus name
3. Bad luck powers, pursuing my life, backfire, in the name of Jesus Christ.
4. O God arise, empower me with wisdom and blessings in the name of Jesus Christ.
5. Evil rain assigned against my glory, dry up by fire, in the name of Jesus.
6. I reverse every satanic exchange of my virtues, glory, and destiny, in the name of Jesus.
7. I renounce every evil covenants, vows, and dedication made upon my life in Jesus name.

8. I break all the curses attached to these evil covenants, in the name of Jesus.
9. Wicked powers from my foundation trading with my goodness, die, in Jesus name.
10. Environmental forces caging my life, scatter by fire, in the name of Jesus.
11. Every owner of the load of sicknesses, poverty and shame, carry your load away in Jesus name.
12. Demoting powers of my father's house release me and die, in the name of Jesus.
13. Demoting powers of my mother's house release me and die, in the name of Jesus.
14. You the pharaoh of my father's house, release me by fire, in the name of Jesus
15. I stand against all satanic attachments that may seek to confuse my decision, in the name of Jesus.

CHAPTER EIGHT

Power To Overcome Fear

Fear is uneasiness of the mind caused by thoughts of impending evil occurrence. It is a strong emotion experienced in anticipation of some specific pain or danger. When God spoke to Abraham in ***Genesis 15:1*** *He said,* ***"Do not be afraid, Abram. I am your shield, your exceedingly great reward."*** Isaiah 54:14 says "You shall be far from oppression; for you shall not fear: and from terror; for it shall not come near you." When Apostle Paul lamented that a wide door and effectual was opened unto him but, there were many adversaries (1 Corinthians 16:9); the major adversary to his success was fear. It was Fear that stole the miracle of Peter when Jesus empowered him to walk on water. But, Peter was terrified by the wind and he began to sink because of fear. Fear causes failure, misfortune and shame. The children of Israel who went with Joshua to spy the land of Canaan died because of fear. The power of fear can destroy your courage and peace in life. It will tell you that the enemies are too strong for you. The voice of fear speaks hopelessness, worry and confusion to the human heart. I pray that any voice of fear speaking against your joy shall be silenced forever in the name of Jesus Christ.

Luke 1:74 confirms that we should serve God without fear. Fearful emotions are always tormenting; it troubles the heart and weakens the body. Hebrews 11:6 says that without faith it is impossible to please God. Fear is a spirit that Satan uses to overcome and rule the heart of man. The spirit of fear is not from God; it is a spirit from the devil which comes to steal your peace, terminates your joy and destroy your destiny***. 2 Timothy 1:7 "God have not given us the spirit of fear, but of power and of love and of a sound mind."*** Fear is a feeling of agitation and anxiety caused by the presence or imagination of danger. Anything you fear is wrongly believed to be stronger and able to punish you. Fear is the enemy that comes like a flood to sweep away your faith (Isaiah 59:19). Whatever you fear is permitted to rule your life.

The fearful will always envisage difficulties and obstacles on the way. Fear has the capacity to enslave and hold your heart captive in the pit of worry. Romans 8:15 confirms that fear is the spirit of bondage and it is not for the children of God. It causes sadness and insecurity. Fear will always tell you that evil is about to happen. It will expose your deficiencies and subdue your strength. A fearful heart will wrongly imagine the destructive possibilities and strength of the enemy. It will make you forget the abilities that God has bestowed upon your life. A fearful person cannot achieve remarkable success in any human endeavor. Bible says "Guard your heart with all diligence because out of it are the issues of life". Fear is a stronghold that torments the heart; it weakens the muscle and destroys your courage. If you always expect negative things to happen, you invariably magnetize evil to yourself. Fear is spiritual invasion assigned to vandalize your destiny. It short-circuits your liberty and pollutes the joy that Jesus secured for you on the cross at Calvary. Fear is the demon of pestilence attached to arrest and deflate the heart and minds. The worst arrow of distress is fear; it makes you unworthy of your right and push you to relinquish your destiny. The fearful heart glorifies the enemy; hence, cannot receive from God.

John 14:1 "Let your heart not be troubled; believe in God and in Jesus Christ." It means that those who believe in God should not allow fear or worry into their heart. Fear leads to shame and untimely death. Fear will cause you to make foolish mistakes due to confusion and aversion in your mind. The Spirit of fear will not allow you to appreciate the greatness of God's love towards you. Holy bible warns that the fearful and the unbelieving will be cast into hell fire. Those who fear the enemy are always troubled on every side. Fear will make you forget your right to the victory that blood of Jesus has purchased for you. Do you know that satanic agents spread fearful information to weaken the faith of their targets? All satanic agents are the chaff in the earth; they frame-up stories to destroy your courage because they are masters of mischief.

Fear is deceptive and it subjects people to negative commands, oppressions and poverty. Some people are just fearful without knowing what they are actually afraid of. Fear is a slave driver of the human heart. ***Hebrew 2:15 "God release those who through fear of death were all***

their lifetime subject to bondage." Are you afraid that the problems in your family will never be solved? Are you frightened by the kind of dreams you had? Is the spirit of fear telling you that you will soon die? I pray for you, that the Spirit of Life in Christ Jesus shall set you free from the bondage of fear and death in Jesus name. 'Fear not' is written 365 times in the Holy Bible; that is, one for each day in the whole year. It is wrong for your heart to be subjected to unbearable fears, because of unpleasant encounters of the past. Satan is responsible for the bad memories that come to people's mind; he uses negative records to becloud your heart in regrets and despair. Persistent fear can open evil doors to sickness, depression and madness of the heart. The devil has a file on all our weak areas, failures and disabilities. It is dangerous to allow fear to rule your life. Everyone is a victim of whatever he fears. The devil manipulates people with fear in order to regulate and ridicule their destiny. The fearful heart is vulnerable to defeat and untimely death. You must decisively condemn negative thoughts and imaginations subjecting your heart to worry and fear. Faith is the victory that overcomes the world; but fear victimizes.

MAJOR PROBLEMS CAUSED BY FEAR

Fear is an unpleasant strong emotion caused by perceived threat or awareness of danger. The devil's kingdom is built on fear while God's kingdom is built on faith. "Whatever is not from faith is sin" (Romans 14:23b). The spirit of fear is stronger than witchcraft. It is the spirit that leads to affliction, poverty and suicide. The Power of fear can paralyze our minds, wills and emotions. God has given us the authority to rule over anything that is not of Him. Fear weakens our prayer life and hinders us from walking in God's love. A man's problem is enlarged and strengthened by fear. Your future is determined by who you choose to obey. If you obey God, your life will not bow to the object of your fear. As Christians, the Lord is the light of our salvation and strength of our lives; only Him deserves our worship and veneration.

Faith will cause you to be in alignment with God, but fear will separate you from light of God. The dangerous power of fear made Adam to hide from the presence of God (Genesis 3:10). When fear entered into the heart of Adam, it pushed him away from God. After Adam ate the forbidden fruit, the first character he exhibited was fear. When God asked him ***"Adam where art you?"*** He said, ***"I heard your voice in the garden and I was afraid so, I hide myself."*** Fear is a spiritual attack designed by the devil to subjugate and annihilate your destiny.

Most of the hassles and troubles in this life are instigated by fear. Those who consult oracles are beclouded by problems caused by fear. Take note that if you magnify your problems as a result of fear, you will not have the courage to confront it. There is no problem on earth that God cannot solve. Those who experienced worst problems are the same people that encountered the greatest miracles. If Joseph was not cast into prison, he would not have become a prime minister in Egypt. Adversities are stepping stones to advancements in life. If Daniel was not cast into the lion's den, he would not have achieved the victory of becoming the Governor. Oppositions are master keys that unlock great opportunities. Remember that Elijah had to contest with the prophets of Baal, before he could prove to the world that his God answers by fire. ***Psalm 91:15 "God will be with you in trouble; he will deliver you and honor you."*** He delivered Paul and Silas from prison. He delivered Shadrach, Meshach and Abednego from furnace of fire.

All these people were not afraid in their troubles; they trusted God and He appeared for them with His mighty power of deliverance. It is time for you to receive the Faith of Jesus Christ, which is able to justify and empower your life. Are you frightened by the circumstances around you? It is a satanic agenda to distract you from the right track to your solutions. Fear will tell you that your problems have defied solutions. It will prevent you from spending enough time to study and meditate on the word of God. The spirit of fear will torment the heart into destructive premonitions. Fear sees only the natural realm but, the power of God's salvation and deliverance is supernatural. The awareness of the enemy should draw you closer to God, like Jehoshaphat; but some people die in fear before the real problem manifests.

Your victory in life is determined by your attitude towards the obstacles you face. The Israelites had to pass through the red sea and wilderness before getting to their promise land. You need to understand that problems are major bridges to our provisions in life. The fearful are disconnected from the move of God's power. God advised Joshua to be courageous because the faint-hearted does not win the battles of life. Faith releases the finger of God to heal, save, and deliver from deep troubles. Some difficult situations are expecting the practice of your faith in Christ. The Just shall live by faith; and the only way to receive from God is through Faith. The sons of God can only manifest when they put faith in action. Fear is a thief that steals the peace of God from our hearts. It kills the joy of living and quenches the fire of revival. It was fear of death that caused Abraham to deny his wife; he told Abimelech that Sarah was his sister (Genesis 20:1-6). Fear has the capacity to weaken the heart and even saps energy from the whole body. It will remind you of all past failures and convince you that there is no hope.

Fearful people ignorantly neglect God and forsake the kindness of God in their life. When fear overtakes your heart, it sends constant threats to make you forget past testimonies of God's love. Bible says "the very hairs on your head are all numbered. So don't be afraid..." (Matthew 10:30). Fear causes shame, nakedness and death. It turns prosperity to poverty. Bible says that 'Joy of the Lord is our strength'. If you allow fear to destroy your joy, it will also destroy your spiritual strength and decay your bones. The power of fear separates people from directions of the Holy Spirit. The Psalmist prayed 'Restore unto me the Joy of salvation and take not thy Holy Spirit from me. A lot of people give undeserved respect to their enemies due to fear. Jesus said "Wherever your treasure is, there shall your mind be". It means that your mind should only be focused on those things that deserve your respect. Your problem does not deserve your fear, do not dwell on them because God has promised you His safety and provisions.

Fear is so dangerous that it can subject a person's soul to the prison of grave powers. ***Psalm 49:15 "But, God will redeem my soul from the power of the grave."*** I pray that the resurrection power of God will deliver you from the dungeon of fear in Jesus name.

Fear is a sin-Romans 14:23 "whatsoever is not of faith is sin" Faith assumes the presence of God and availability of His power to turn situations around, but fear assumes the absence of God. The Lord declares his Love and Mercy for you, but Satan says, you are unworthy of God's kindness. F.E.A.R. is an acronym representing 'False Evidence Appearing Real.' A vast majority of the things we fear will never become reality. Fear will prevent you from praying in faith and cause you to doubt God.

James 1:6-7 advises that the doubtful mind will not receive anything from God. A double minded man is unstable in all his ways. The devil understands spiritual laws and specific penalties, so he uses the spirit of fear to deprive people of their rightful blessings. The spirit of fear can demote, steal and overthrow glorious destiny. ***Ephesians 6:12 "For we do not wrestle against flesh and blood, but against principalities, against powers, against the rulers of the darkness of this age, against spiritual hosts of wickedness in the heavenly places."*** Fear will empower your enemies to pursue you when they are supposed to flee from you. Fear will release the spirit of guilt and unworthiness upon you. The gospel of Christ terminates fear and empower Christians to achieve the promises of God. It is important to note that every promising child must pass through problems before achieving God's provision for his life. Your problems will reveal some hidden capabilities to help you fulfill the purposes of God.

Faith is a feeling of absolute confidence that God will do exactly what He has spoken in His words. A man will never be great really, until he faces challenges, oppositions and obstacles in life. There is always a story behind every glory. If you have not experienced distress, you will not understand that God is a comforter. In 2 Timothy 3:12 Paul informed Timothy that ***"All who desire to live godly in Christ Jesus will suffer persecution."*** Without persecution, you will not trust God as your great deliverer. It is necessary to overlook your problems and keep thanking God because he has promised solutions in abundance for you. You may have no control over what comes to you, but you can decide how you will react to it.

When the enemy notice that attacks against you, are making you stronger and closer to God; they will leave you alone. Anything that draws you closer to God provides the privilege of salvation and overwhelming glory. As you need to squeeze the orange in order enjoy the juice; settle it in your heart that plots of the enemy will increase your spiritual power and fellowship with the God that answers by fire. If Paul and Silas had felt defeated in the prison, the earthquake of deliverance would not have appeared for them.

DELIVERANCE FROM THE POWER OF FEAR

Psalm 34:4 "I sought the Lord, and He heard me, and delivered me from all my fears." Faith is the consistency of seeking God despite the prevailing circumstances. It is the key to access the spiritual realm and unlock heavenly blessings. Faith is proof of existence of something that is not tangible to natural senses. But fear undermines all scriptural truths. Faith and fear are persistent belief in an unseen future. Fears are thoughts that oppose the promises of God; but faith authorizes you to receive the performance of God's promises for your life. Bible says ***"Put on the whole armor of God so that you will be able to stand firm against all strategies of the devil" Ephesians 6:11.*** You must fill your heart with the word of God, which is the sword of the Spirit. The contests between faith and fear exists in critical moments in every life; your submission to one means vehement resistance to the other. ***James 4:7 "Submit yourself to God, resist the devil and he will flee from you."*** This means that your submission to God is obvious declaration that the devil has no place in your life; then he will flee. ***"Isaiah 41:10-11 Fear not, for I am with you; be not dismayed, for I am your God. I will strengthen you, Yes, I will help you, I will uphold you with My righteous right hand.' "Behold, all those who were incensed against you shall be ashamed and disgraced; they shall be as nothing, and those who strive with you shall perish."*** Be strong in the Lord and in the power of His might. Fear is the most fatal weapon of the devil; it has wasted many lives in their prime. Those ordained for greatness have failed woefully and regrettably defeated, because of fear.

The spirit of fear deprives people from daily peace and joy of life. If you do not meditate on the word of God, the enemy will manipulate your emotions, thoughts and imaginations. It captures your mind to instigate destructive and lamentable actions. ***2 Corinthians 10:3-5 "For though we walk in the flesh, we do not war according to the flesh. For the weapons of our warfare are not carnal but mighty in God for pulling down strongholds, casting down arguments and every high thing that exalts itself against the knowledge of God, bringing every thought into captivity to the obedience of Christ."*** Fear deludes the heart with disgraceful thoughts and hopeless decisions. It says that you are in danger and that your marriage will not get better. Fear discourages you from taking bold steps towards converting your vision to reality in life. It reduces you to seek advice from wrong people. Fear tells you that you have lost the final opportunity so there is no hope for you anymore. The fearful heart will never be organized or composed. Fear is a lethal missile of the devil and his agents. Satan manipulates people's dreams at night in order to make them afraid. Fear is a manifestation of the kingdom of darkness. Dream confusions have become one of the most functional weapon of the devil to intimidate people. Word of God is the only knowledge that will truly deliver you from the oppressive power of fear. David said, **"Whenever I am afraid, I will trust in You." (Psalm 56:3).** Fear says the opposite of what God says. The strongman of fear must be defeated before achievement of great destinies. The power of God inside of believers is greater than all negative situations in the world. We must look steadfastly unto Jesus, the author and finisher of our faith.

Once you allow fear to separate you from God, the enemy will take advantage to punish and shatter the person's life. ***"If anyone does not abide in Me, he is cast out as a branch and is withered; and they gather them and throw them into the fire, and they are burned." John 15:6*** Several lives have ended abruptly and disgracefully because of fear. It was the intimidating power of fear that made Peter to deny Jesus Christ. Some couples looking for children have wasted millions of money to fake prophets and herbalists because of fear of the unknown. The dangerous power of fear has compelled some wives to diabolic practices in order to keep their marriages. Most idol worshippers are subjected to intense fear on daily basis. Fear will make you to become slaves to fake pastors and prophets.

When you understand the truth of the gospel; which confirms you as son of God (John 1:12); you will no longer be at the mercies of fake prophets, confusing people with terrifying visions. When you acknowledge the abundance of God's Love upon your life; then you will not be afraid when human beings hate you. The people causing problems for you may not know that they are training you to be stronger. ***Job 5:12 "God will frustrate the devices of the crafty, so that their hands cannot carry out their wicked plans."*** There is no victory without battles, no triumph without trials and no champion without competitions. As long as Jesus

Christ is your shepherd, your mistakes will not end you in a mess rather it will attract miracles to you.

When Jonah was in the belly of fish, he kept praying and God delivered him. Every problem in life has a solution; unless you give up in your mind, you will never fail. The trouble of life does not negate the power of God's deliverance. If you spend most time of your life in fear and thinking about your enemies, when will you have time for God and for the fulfillment of your destiny. Jesus says "For this reason, Son of God was manifested that He shall destroy the works of darkness." The Spirit of God ensured the resurrection of Jesus Christ so that He will destroy all the powers that are troubling your life. Because Jesus has resurrected, our problems must be buried in the grave. You must be careful of what you do with your mind, attention and time. Your problem and your enemies does not worth the time that you waste thinking about them. Free your mind from your problems and focus your attention on our Lord Jesus Christ. **James 5:13 "If anyone is afflicted or troubled; let him pray".** Whenever you are troubled, the best step to take is prayer. ***Bible says "Call upon God in the day of trouble, He will deliver you and you shall glorify Him".***

LIVING ABOVE FEAR

Your faith in the steadfast love of Christ is best antidote to fear regardless of your circumstances. ***So we may boldly say: "The Lord is my helper; I will not fear. What can man do to me?" Hebrews 13:6.*** We must continually obey and trust in availability of God's power to intervene in our situations. The satanic power of fear has pushed people to committing suicide. In fact, all suicidal tendencies in human thoughts are caused by fear. When the voice of fear tells you that there is no hope of solution to your problems; it will instigate you to catastrophic actions. The word of God in your heart will steer up the passion to trust in Him. The power of fear is capable of darkening the thoughts, and eyes of any man. Fear is the major cause of spiritual blindness; fearful heart cannot receive visions from heaven. Fear will make you to obey satanic instructions and cause you to serve evil men. The spirit of fear can separate a man from his destiny and sentence him to the abyss of depression and distress. Fear leads to insecurity and keeps the heart in the dungeon of apprehension. It is an offence to God when a person subjects his heart to fear because of threats from another man.

Isaiah 51:12-13 "I, even I, am He who comforts you. Who are you that you should be afraid of a man who will die, and of the son of a man who will be made like grass? And you forget the Lord your Maker, who stretched out the heavens and laid the foundations of the earth. You have feared continually every day because of the fury of the oppressor, when he has prepared to destroy. And where is the fury of the oppressor? Most threats that subjects people to fear, will never come to pass. Even the man who is threatening you is afraid of you. If you love God and walk in His righteousness, you must not fear. Fear is baseless information from the kingdom of darkness, which invades a person's heart with the agenda to distract his actions and kill his courage. Any information that contradicts the word of God should not germinate in your life. Everyone is a victim of whatever he fears. Those who found shelter in God's secret place are covered under the shadow of His wings. This is habitation of absolute safety; the eternal God is our refuge. We shall not be afraid of the terror by night nor the arrow that flies in the day. The works and weapons of the enemy is under our feet, as defeated foe.

All Christians should be trained in spiritual warfare, with the knowledge to fight the battles of life through prayers. Our God is a man of war; the Lord is His name. The captain of our salvation, Jesus Christ, revealed the necessity of casting out demons and defeating all oppositions. We should pray targeted prayers that will put our spiritual enemies to flight and terminate all inherited afflictions on assignment to short-circuit our destinies. Another cause of apprehension in people's heart is trusting on fellow human beings for major breakthroughs in life. The Psalmist declared ***"As long as I live, I will praise the Lord; I will sing praises to my God while I have my being. Do not put your trust in princes, nor in a son of man, in whom there is no help." Psalm 146:2-3.*** People's heart departs from the Lord due to unyielding trust in another man. Only God can help and honor you genuinely because in vain is the honor of man. It is better to trust in the Lord than to put confidence in man. Unless a helper is ordained by God, he can disappoint you but, the power of God whom you serve will always have better replacement. Blessed is the man who trusts in the Lord, and whose hope is the Lord. If you look for perfect love in relationships of the flesh, you will get disappointments. The only place where you can experience perfect love is in an intimate relationship with your Heavenly Father. You must allow the light of the glorious gospel of Jesus Christ to shine in your heart. If you can endeavor to read Holy Bible on daily basis, at least one hour per day, regularly for one month; you will be surprised that most of your fears will disappear miraculously.

PRAYER POINTS:

1. Any battle from my father's house raging against my life, die by fire in Jesus name.
2. Holy Ghost fire, arise, disconnect my life from evil yokes in Jesus name.
3. My life arises, receive the faith to live above fear and confusions of life in Jesus name.
4. Any wicked hand planting evil things into my life during the hours of my sleep be cut off by the sword of God in the name of Jesus.
5. Powers performing sacrifices to rubbish my destiny, catch fine and die in Jesus name.
6. Any witchcraft hand digging evil pits against my life, die in your pit in Jesus name.
7. Spirit of the living God, possess my life to execute your purposes on earth in Jesus name.
8. Any power manipulating my life from evil altars be demolished by fire, in Jesus name.
9. Unseen hands from my foundation, stealing the fruits of my labour, I bring the judgment of God against you, disappear by fire in the Mighty Name of Jesus Christ.
10. Ancestral covenants and dedications working against my life die by fire, in the name of Jesus Christ.
11. O God arise, afflict my afflictions and oppress my oppressors in the name of Jesus Christ.
12. O God, deliver me from the workers of iniquity and save me from bloody men in Jesus name.

13. I stand against all satanic attachments that may seek to confuse my decision, in the name of Jesus.
14. I receive special wisdom from God to open doors of miracles and riches in the name of Jesus Christ.
15. Lord, make my life a miracle and be glorified in every area of it, in the name of Jesus Christ. AMEN.

CHAPTER NINE

Freedom From Foundational Limitations

Human actions and covenants are spiritual plants that its lifespan transcend to subsequent generations. The seed planted by your actions today will germinate and bear fruits that your children must embrace; either positively or negatively. The works of your hand can either plant blessings or curses that will definitely affect successive generations of your lineage. A person's covenant with God will benefit his children while dedications to idols will trouble and limit the offspring. Limitations are boundaries set by the enemy to restrain a person in the spirit realm. Most circumstances of life are orchestrated from the spirit realm; they are planned and executed by invisible forces, using the collections of ancestral deeds to regulate the destinies of children. This is the reason why some families pass through hurtful mysterious circumstances. Prayer is crucial because only God can deliver from strange events that affect family members.

The Children of Israel received great deliverance because their fathers had covenant with God.

God explained the reason for helping the Israelites in ***Deuteronomy 7:8 "The Lord loves you, because He would keep the oath which He swore to your fathers, the Lord has brought you out with a mighty hand, and redeemed you from the house of bondage, from the hand of Pharaoh king of Egypt."*** God decided to deliver the children of Israel because of His covenant with their fathers. The key to deliverance from foundational limitation is covenant with God. Foundational powers are the strong oppressors in your father's house assigned to ensure that you live in conformity with the evil pattern of your ancestors. Those who make covenant with idols subject their children to the negative consequences of their mistakes.

There is a powerful relationship between your foundation and your destiny. Your foundation determines how you live and what you achieve in the land of the living. Shriners perform sacrifices on behalf of themselves and their children; dedicating the family line to idols will attract curses against the children. If your ancestors shed innocent blood, it will be problematic foundation because slain blood would be crying against the off springs in the family. The spirit of limitation from the foundation can delay and resist a destiny from getting to ordained positions of glory. Salvation gives you the weapon and privilege to fight and deliver your destiny from foundational bondages. Most problems are like weeds that has its root in the foundation of a person. As the strength of a building is determined by its foundation, deeds of parents and ancestry play significant roles in different stages of people's lives. Your ancestry is spiritual foundation that influences and dominates various aspects of your life. Two different people from separate foundation may face similar battles; but one can be delivered while the other is consumed. This is because the spiritual hands that holds the foundational pillars of their lives are different. The life of a man usually tilts to the pattern of his fathers. Most times, women encounter similar experiences that their mother suffered in marriages.

Spiritually speaking, there are two destinies in the life of everyone. Your first destiny is the blueprint of God for your life, which carries heavenly projects for your generation. This embodies the promises of God and His divine calendar for your life. The second destiny is the ridiculous position designed by the strongman of darkness in your foundation. They struggle to enforce shameful ancestral pattern against a person throughout his lifetime; unless and until you pray seriously to deliver yourself from them. The strongman of darkness wants to uphold the judgement of your father's mistakes upon your life; they enforce curses and idolatrous dedications in the family line. When Ahab offended God, Prophet Elijah was sent to declare terrible curses against him. But surprisingly, Ahab humbled himself and God told the Prophet that the curses and calamitous consequences of Ahab's offence will be suffered by his children. ***1 Kings 21:28 And the word of the Lord came to Elijah the Tishbite, saying, "See how Ahab has humbled himself before Me? Because he has humbled himself before Me, I will not bring the calamity in his days. In the days of his***

son I will bring the calamity on his house." The deeds of your fathers can determine your ascension to throne of glory or dissension to abject penury. Whatever you do today, is sowing seeds to the future of your children. Your positive expression of love, integrity and generosity to mankind will be enjoyed by your children. The good things you do presently will greatly profit your children in future. Your deeds of kindness and integrity will be registered in the spirit realm and will definitely produce divine help and protection for the fruits of your loins.

LIMITING POWERS OF YOUR FATHER'S HOUSE

Limiting powers are strong agents of darkness which reduces and hinders people from greatness.

They are invisible tough powers that supervises negative circumstances in the family. To be limited means to be restricted, obstructed and restrained. These powers disqualify members of the family from all forms of comforts including finances, health, marriages, talents and investments. They are powers that transport ailments, disabilities and misfortunes from generation to generation in the lineage. They battle against your divine allocation of glorious settlements in the spirit realm. The men, women and youths in a family ordinarily follows a pattern designed and enforced from the spirit realm. Things that happen in our physical lives are manifestations of spiritual conclusions. If you discuss with some people with diabetes, you will be surprised to discover that one of the parents or grand-parents suffered diabetes. Foundational powers carry-over spiritual afflictions like untimely death, poverty, wrong marriages, evil habits in children, anger and idolatry; to next generations. The Almighty God has divine purpose for every family. Also, foundational limiting powers have its own wicked agenda for the family. Therefore, it becomes a battle if you must align with the vision of God for your life. The idols worshipped by ancestors can impose a ridiculous foundation against a destiny. Ancestral iniquities and inclinations can detain a person's glory in the kingdom of darkness. The main battle of life is to translate from foundational disorder to the divinely ordained pattern for your destiny. ***Colossians 1:13-14 "He has delivered us from the power of darkness and conveyed us into the kingdom of the Son of His love, in whom we have redemption through His blood,***

the forgiveness of sins." Some people ignorantly disregards the essence of foundational battles just because they have financial successes, but the battle may be fiercely raging in other areas of their lives. Some men in the family go through similar problems in marriages while the battle in another family may be sicknesses, and others may be battling with accidents, untimely deaths and violence or hatred among siblings. Every family needs to draw nearer to God in prayers.

This scripture confirms that battles against destinies are enforced by the powers of darkness. ***Ephesians 6:12 "We wrestle, not against flesh and blood, but against principalities, against powers, against the rulers of darkness of this world, and against spiritual wickedness in high places."*** These powers are rulers in the dark world. They govern wicked agents as executioners of evil projects, and they also occupy position of spiritual authority. The Bible further explains that same evil powers wrestle with human beings. They enslave people in the bondage of fear, diverse afflictions and terrible patterns in the family line. They enforce parental dedications and ancestral covenants to keep people in mysterious oppressions. These strong enemies draw authority from the iniquity of the fathers who had offended God or made covenants with idols. The foundational limiting powers subjugate people's destinies into destructive captivity caused by idolatrous dedications in the lineage. These wicked powers challenge divine purposes by questioning the glory of God from settling in the family. They build evil ancient gates that imprison destinies; and deprive the manifestation of great talents in the family. Psalms 24:7 the voice of God commanded them saying ***"Lift up your heads O ye gates and lift them up, ye everlasting doors; and the King of Glory shall come in."*** But they questioned **"Who is this King of Glory?"** The fact that wicked powers stay in high places means they operate with some level of spiritual authority. These are powers of the mighty that inflicts terrible wickedness against the souls of men. They claim ownership of the souls because earlier generations have acquiesced the land through sacrifices and covenants to powers of darkness. This is why they questioned the King of Glory. Ancient spiritual landlord powers do not vacate a territory without serious battle. Hence, God announced Himself thus "The Lord strong and mighty, the Lord mighty in battle." You must fight and defeat them spiritually before they can be dislodged from your foundation. The strongman of darkness wrongly claims the original right of possession to the foundations of families and communities. **Psalm 24:10 declares "The Lord of Host is the King of Glory."** The One who exists before the foundation was laid, the Alpha and Omega, the source and founder of all ancient creations. The best way to deliver your glory from foundational siege of darkness is by inviting the Lord of Host. Our God is a man of war; the Lord is His name.

1. NEGATIVE SPIRITUAL ENVIRONMENTS

Irrespective of the physical location of a person, his spirit man can still connect to the environment of his origin. As the blood and genes of your ancestors' flow in your veins, their traits and spiritual liabilities also flow in your life. There are executors of evil projects and enforcers of evil judgments in families and communities. They avenge the iniquities of ancestors upon their children. They determine the next person to die and enforce dark rulership in people's lives; they keep evil register for the family. No wonder the Bible says "deliver them who are appointed to die" (Psalms 79:11). These foundational wicked powers lead people into fatal and lamentable relationships. They wire your heart to love and trust the wrong person who will frustrate and distress your life. These wicked activities are executed by strongman of darkness in the foundation of a person's destiny.

The strongman of darkness is the foundational power that entrap destinies, regulates glory and subjugate lives. The same way that ancestors of Moses took them to Egypt, where the children of Israel were born and found themselves under the tyranny of Pharaoh; spiritual oppressors are dark powers in the foundation working against your destiny because of the mistakes of your ancestors, agreements of your fathers and iniquities of your fore-parents. They oppose your rightful possessions and negatively influence good things that belong to you. The principalities of darkness in the foundation can pass terrible judgments against lives and sentence them to death in the spirit realm. We need to pray to become the battle axe that God will use to destroy ancestral strongholds. Deliverance prayer is the weapon to destroy foundational strongman and possess our destined inheritance. Strongman is the manager of evil warehouse, the chief ancestral demon. It is the leader of congregation of evil powers. ***Luke 11:21-22 "When a strongman armed, keepeth his palace, his good are in peace; but when a stronger than he shall come upon him and overcome him, he taketh from him all his armour wherein he trusteth and divideth his spoils."*** All the goods in the spiritual palace of the strong man originally belonged to members of the family; but stolen and impounded by the strongman of darkness.

They swallow riches, talents, gifts; and hinder ordained helpers so that the family will not lift up their heads. The strongman is fully armed; means they are battle ready. Even before confiscating the stars, wealth and glory of the family, they had defeated earlier generations and stolen their possession. Only deliverance prayers will vindicate and empower you to recover your possessions. The Strongman of darkness uses remote control powers to distract, distress and mislead people. You need the stronger man, Jesus Christ, to overcome and take away the armor from the strongman of darkness. Then, the benefits in the storehouse will be graciously distributed to members of the family. The commodities in the store house are divinely ordained benefits which include but not limited to: helpers, riches, virtues, wisdom, health, good children and opportunities for glorious testimonies. A lot of spiritual transactions are sealed in the dreams, as your spirit man consents through evil food, drinks and dark covenants while asleep. You need to charge your spirit man with fire of the Holy Ghost to enable you overcome night raiders and prevent them from booking dark appointments against your life in the spirit realm. God will pull you out from the dustbin of life; satanic powers will not use you to settle their accounts.

2. DANGER OF BLOOD GUILTINESS

Psalm 51:14 "Deliver me from the guilt of bloodshed, O God, the God of my salvation, and my tongue shall sing aloud of Your righteousness." Blood guiltiness means iniquity caused by bloodshed. If your parents or ancestors shed innocent blood, it would cry to God like the blood of Abel, seeking for vengeance. The blood continues to cry because its untimely death also truncated the lives and destinies of children the person would have produced. This gives the strongman of darkness the authority to oppress several generations of people in the family. Sometimes, it causes violent death because the murdered blood calls for retaliation through death. It will subject children of the killer to abject poverty, vagabond attitudes, constant failures, frustrations and confusions. Apart from legal culpability or penalty for murder, the spiritual punishment is excruciatingly painful. Hence, we must advice everyone to avoid any form of violence, anger or crisis capable of causing death.

Slain blood defiles the land against the inhabitants. It attracts the wrath of God upon the offspring and pursues them into the abyss of apprehension, curses and tragic occurrences.

God specifically warned the Israelites that whenever they found dead corpse lying in the field, and it is not known who killed him, they must wash their hands to free their land from blood of the slain. ***Deuteronomy 21:7-9 "Then they shall answer and say, 'Our hands have not shed this blood, nor have our eyes seen it. Provide atonement, O Lord, for Your people Israel, whom You have redeemed, and do not lay innocent blood to the charge of Your people Israel.' And atonement shall be provided on their behalf for the blood. So you shall put away the guilt of innocent blood from among you when you do what is right in the sight of the Lord."***

The guilt of innocent blood is endemic, catastrophic and destructive to families and communities. When Pontius Pilate washed his hands, he declared "I am innocent of the blood of this just man." It means that a person can either be innocent or guilty of the blood of the slain. The guilt of blood can cause tragedy against the people from one generation to another.

In Matthew 27:25 All the people answered and said, ***"His blood be on us and on our children."*** On the day that Jesus was crucified, the crowd accepted the guilt of blood to be upon them and upon their children. In such manner, earlier generations have ignorantly consented to shedding of innocent blood. It is essential to pray for deliverance from the blood guiltiness of your ancestors.

You need to call on the precious Blood of Jesus Christ that speaks better things than blood of Abel, to silence any blood crying against your greatness from your foundation. There is no accident or emergency in the spirit realm. Any time people die in multitudes, it is usually the consequence of crying blood. Killing an innocent person can subject the whole community into bondage of afflictions, shame and mysterious destructions.

Murderers are liable to die untimely and wretched because they are rebels in the sight of God. It is written that "the rebellious dwell in dry land." And, their sin is like that of witchcraft who has lost the rights to live. ***"Thou shall not allow a witch to live" Exodus 22:18.*** God hears the voice of innocent blood whenever it cries to Him for vengeance. Shedding of blood will incur the violent anger of God to punish everything that belongs to the murderer.

Jesus paid with his blood to deliver humanity from sin. Blood is the greatest sacrifice on earth.

2 Kings 3:26-27 ***"And when the king of Moab saw that the battle was too fierce for him, he took with him seven hundred men who drew swords, to break through to the king of Edom, but they could not. Then he took his eldest son who would have reigned in his place, and offered him as a burnt offering upon the wall; and there was great indignation against Israel. So they departed from him and returned to their own land."*** The King of Moab was severely being defeated by Israelites in the battle; he first took seven hundred trained soldiers but failed. Then, he killed his first son by the wall, and Israel fled. Shedding of his son's blood changed the equation because of the spiritual power in blood sacrifice. Shedding of innocent blood gives authority to dark powers to inflict pains and destructions against a family. Christians need to seriously pray for the blood of Jesus to purge our foundations because of the idolatrous traditions of our ancestors. The ancient slave trade and killing of twins caused many innocent blood to cry.

Blood shed has serious penalties and calamitous consequences. God requires the blood from the hands of the murderers. Matthew 27:4 Judas said that he **"sinned by betraying innocent blood;"** afterwards, he hanged himself. Also, the chief priest referred to the thirty pieces of silver as **"the price of blood"** and declared that **"it is not lawful to put them into the treasury."** They bought a field with it and called it **"the field of blood."**

Some people may be doing very well, but immediately they relocate to a particular house, their business collapses, the wealth begin to diminish until they lose everything and begin to beg for basic needs. Bible says that the price of blood should not be put into the treasury, meaning that any money that emanates from blood shed is cursed. If it is used to build house, the compound will be plagued with misfortune and catastrophe. If a person kills by diabolic means, occultism, armed robbery, kidnapping, assassination for money or killing for political reasons; anything built with such money must be doomed in incessant woes. They always end in jeopardy because of the crying blood. Many people who kill their colleagues or political associates because of position always suffer terminal illness before they die empty. Shedding of blood is the oldest and most heinous sin of mankind. God supervises the judgement! At times, he permits foundational strongman to punish the killers from one generation to the other until justice is properly served. Some occult practitioners and ritual killers who sacrifice the blood of relatives in order to acquire riches will end in misery and wretchedness. The only benefit of life is to seek God and hate every evil way. Only the blessing of God is totally free from destructive attachments. ***Romans 8:32 "He who did not spare His own Son, but delivered Him up for us all, how shall He not with Him also freely give us all things?"*** If you serve God and keep His commandments, He will graciously deliver you from foundational liabilities and uplift you to greatness beyond imaginations. The earth is the Lord's and the fullness thereof; silver and God belongs to Him.

3. GENERATIONAL TRANSFER OF JUDGEMENTS

Hebrews 7:9-10 "Even Levi, who receives tithes, paid tithes through Abraham, so to speak, for he was still in the loins of his father when Melchizedek met him." Levi was the third generation of Abraham but surprisingly, the Bible says that because he was in the loins of Abraham, when Abraham paid tithe to Melchizedek; that he (Levi) also paid tithe in Abraham. This proves that you spiritually participated in the deeds of your ancestors because you were in their loins when they performed the evil acts; hence deliverance is greatly needed. This means that you must pray to deliver yourself from the idolatrous activities, horrible traditions and covenants of ancestors.

What your grandfathers did before you were born can be connected to your life, unless and until you break it off through fervent fire prayers. You need to cry to God to detach you from the oppressions of darkness in your foundation. The stronghold of curses and covenants in the foundation can satanically glue people to evil bus stop. Family members are suppressed in bondages of darkness, caused by sins of ancient fathers.

As Levi was confirmed to have performed exactly what Abraham did even when he was yet unborn, the actions of tithe performed by Abraham was recorded on his name. If Abraham had made covenants with the devil or sacrificed to idol powers, it would be transferred to Levi, spiritually. That is the reason why children of sorcerers, occultists and idolaters experience strange occurrences both in their dreams and in the physical world. The devil that was befriended by parents can become strangers to the lives of the children. The world is so deep that future benefits can be sold-off by dark power. The worst problem in the life of man is entrenched in the foundation. Most people encounter series of stubborn afflictions not because of their sin, but due to the problems inherited from their ancestors. Gideon was from an idolatrous background; his father was the High Priest of Baal. So, God instructed Gideon to destroy his father's altar and build an altar unto God. The solution is total disconnection from foundational evil order, through violent deliverance prayers. ***Matthew 11:12 "And from the days of John the Baptist until now the kingdom of heaven suffers violence, and the violent take it by force."***

4. RELEVANT SPIRITUAL LAWS

Romans 8:2 "For the law of the Spirit of life in Christ Jesus has made me free from the law of sin and death."

Two fundamental laws are identified here:

The first law gives liberty and life while the second law is about bondage, punishment and death.

(i) **Law of the Spirit of Life in Christ Jesus:** This is the law of emancipation, deliverance, mercy and joy of the Holy Ghost. The law of the Spirit of Life in Christ Jesus is the resurrection power that brings to life every good thing that was dead within and around you. It appropriates the efficacy of the word of God to give you the required deliverance and comfort as child of God. This law establishes the kindness of God and enlightens our lives with light that darkness cannot comprehend. It uses the blood of Jesus to nullify handwriting of ordinances which were contrary to us. It possesses the anointing of Holy Ghost that break yokes of limitations, delivers from bondage of the strongman and condemns evil voices speaking against you in judgement.

The Lord Jesus removes dangers, tragedy and troubles from our paths; ancestral dedications are broken away and we are free. This law stands on the finished work of Christ and releases Grace into our lives. It destroys the work of darkness and terminates negative pattern in the foundation.

(ii) **The law of sin and death:** this is the law of bondage, judgment and destruction. It enforces the penalty of death as a result of iniquity. The law of sin and death has no mercy to offenders. Their agents are satanic executioners of evil judgments and arresters of progress.

Psalms 78:63 "The fire consumed their young men, and their maidens were not given in marriage." The law of sin ignites wicked fire that consumes glory and disables men in their youths. The evil spiritual fire are serpents of wastage and scorpions of death that besiege destinies. The handlers of the evil fire are principalities of darkness which terrifies men and stop them from making meaningful progress. They also stop women in the family from enjoying marriages, pushing them to men that would bury the gift of God in their lives. The strongman of darkness in the foundation pushes the women to regrettable and distressful marital lives. Some things that happen to people are exact repetitions of things that had occurred in the past generations of their lineage. The same powers that pushed their fathers to destructive mistakes, still operates against present members of the family and enforces the evil pattern against them. This is called Collective Captivity. You need to passionately connect to the Spirit of God with fervent prayers to deliver yourself from the powers of the mighty and the terrible. God will overturn their contentions fashioned against your glory, and uplift you beyond their oppressions. Spirit of God will overrule dark judgements and establish divine liberty and peace in our lives.

5. HUMAN MIND AS THE BATTLEGROUND

Most times, these powers succeed by besieging and controlling our thoughts and imaginations.

2 Corinthians 10:3-5 "For though we walk in the flesh, we do not war according to the flesh. For the weapons of our warfare are not carnal but mighty in God for pulling down strongholds, casting down arguments and every high thing that exalts itself against the knowledge of God, bringing every thought into captivity to the obedience of Christ." The battleground where the actual war takes place is the mind. The armies of darkness control human thoughts and imaginations. They send evil ideas in form of internal arguments to imprison the mind and subject the person to untold confusions. They persuade people into wrong choices, wasteful actions and lamentable decisions. These are evil voices from the foundation that demote destinies, amputate glory and tarnishes good reputations. They resist the knowledge of God in people's minds, through distractions from prayers and bible study. It opposes the goodness of God by burying people's talents.

These wicked powers relegate people from givers to beggars, and displace them from honor to ridicule. It causes distress, lustful destructive inclinations and downgrades people from grace to grass. They form stronghold in people's mind, besieging their emotions, thoughts and actions. Their weapons are voices of dark judgments, you must condemn them, as written in ***Isaiah 54:17 "No weapon formed against you shall prosper, and every tongue which rises against you in judgment, you shall condemn. This is the heritage of the servants of the Lord, and their righteousness is from Me," Says the Lord.*** These evil voices accuse people at the edge of breakthroughs and separate them from ordained helpers. They can make you to lose interest in the things of God through weakness in fasting and prayers. They give evil food and drinks to people in the dream to obstruct breakthroughs. Some people are subjected to intense fear and worry in their mind, with premonition that something bad is about to happen. Their heart is filled with anxiety, weakness in decisions and inordinate lustful cravings. They persuade people to swiftly act on wrong choices which will later cause severe regrets, uneasiness and painful loss. Their priority is to ensure that your mind dwell in worry, fear and confusion; to prevent you from praising God.

HOW TO BE DELIVERED FROM FOUNDATIONAL LIMITATIONS

1. RIGHT PRAYERS: We need to invite God to possess our land and dispossess the enemy.

   Make the decision to disconnect your life and destiny from the evil orders in your foundation.

   First and foremost, you will accept Jesus Christ as your Lord and savior. Then, incubate your life in the power of Holy Ghost through consistent prayers and study of the word of God. You can do research of your foundation by asking your parents about some activities of your ancestors. Find out some negative trends in the family and pray to disconnect your life and future generations from the trends. Pray the blood of Jesus Christ to purify, liberate and deliver your foundation.

   Psalm 74:20 "Have respect to the covenant; for the dark places of the earth are full of the haunts of cruelty." Limiting powers in the foundation dwell in dark places and all its activities are cruel, merciless and truncation of destinies. You must pray to dislodge the habitation of dark powers in your foundation. Call down the Spirit of God to occupy the foundation of your destiny. Pray that warrior angels from heaven should arrest and destroy the hunters of darkness in your foundation. Pray the Blood of Jesus to deliver you from blood guiltiness; and from judgments of afflictions caused by any of your relatives whether living or dead.

Pray to separate yourself from promises made concerning your life, to any idol, by your parents or ancestors.

At times, people unconsciously pray in the dream and great deliverance happens in their lives. Your tenacious devotions to God will connect your spirit man to the wonderful works of God, and will deliver you from foundational curses and oppressions. Most limitations against destinies are caused by problems in the foundation. You must ask the Holy Ghost to overshadow your dream life. Foundational wasting powers sometimes operate at night, to seal evil transactions against the person's soul. They join people to commune with dead relatives in their dream.

2. PRAY AGAINST THE SPIRIT OF LIMITATION: The destiny of man is a progressive destiny; however certain forces arise to hinder the flow of progress in people's lives. Spirit of limitation can collapse a glorious destiny. There are foundational powers that determines and allocates punishment against men and women of different generations in a family. You must pray to destroy the spirit of limitation; they appear to hinder people at the edge of breakthroughs. They stop helpers from releasing blessings to their victim, and they prepare embargo to stagnate the person's life and finances. Their priority is to make sure that you do not lift up your head.

   Zechariah 1:18-20 "Then I raised my eyes and looked, and there were four horns. And I said to the angel who talked with me, "What are these?" So he answered me, "These are the horns that have scattered Judah, Israel, and Jerusalem." Then the Lord showed me four craftsmen. And I said, "What are these coming to do?" So he said, "These are the horns that scattered Judah, so that no one could lift up his head; but the craftsmen are coming to terrify them, to cast out the horns of the nations that lifted up their horn against the land of Judah to scatter it."
   The spirit of limitation are bearers of evil horns that resist people from rising and shining. They are satanic immigration officers that resists a person from moving to his next level of glory. They make people to perform below their capacity. You need to seriously pray against the spirit that limited your parents and its working

very hard to limit your destiny. You must endeavor to engage in fasting and personally organized program of prayers, using the weapons of warfare available in the scriptures. To effectively pray and overcome the spirit of limitation, you must specifically address the strongman in your foundation, commanding them to release your benefits in their storehouse. You will fervently engage in deliverance and yoke breaking prayers, releasing yourself from ancestral evil yokes, curses, dedications and covenants.

Prayer is the gateway to spiritual liberty, restoration and victory over foundational strongman.

PRAYER POINTS

1. Every task master, assigned against me, somersault and die, in the name of Jesus.
2. Any serpentine spirit, spitting on my breakthrough, roast, in the name of Jesus.
3. Foundational Pharaoh in my life, destroy yourself, in the name of Jesus.
4. Every satanic decision, taken against my progress, be nullified, in the name of Jesus.
5. Overcoming power, dominion prosperity, overshadow my life in the name of Jesus Christ.
6. Every power of darkness, following me about, die, in the name of Jesus.
7. Oh Lord, remove the penalty of judgment upon my life and calling, in Jesus name.
8. Every satanic weapon, formed against my destiny, backfire, in the name of Jesus.
9. Oh Lord, anoint me to recover the wasted years in every area of my life, in Jesus name.
10. Garment of Pharaoh that is upon my life, be removed by fire, in the name of Jesus.
11. Every power that has refused to allow my star to operate, die, in Jesus' name.

12. Every dark handwriting in my foundation, be nullified by fire in Jesus name.
13. Every power assigned to redesign my destiny, die, in the name of Jesus.
14. O God arise and scatter every power that is assigned to stop me, in the name of Jesus.
15. Any strongman standing at my right hand with agenda to stop my blessings, fall down and die in Jesus name.

Printed in the United States
By Bookmasters